101 Great Lowfat Mexican Dishes

Hot, Spicy & Healthful

Margaret Martinez

PRIMA PUBLISHING

For my husband and family

PRIMA PUBLISHING and its colophon, which consists of the letter P over PRIMA, are registered trademarks of Prima Communications, Inc.

Cover photography © 1994 Kent Lacin

Library of Congress Cataloging-in-Publication Data

Martinez, Margaret
    101 great lowfat Mexican dishes: hot, spicy, and healthful / Margaret Martinez.
        p.   cm.
    Includes index.
    ISBN 0-7615-0009-X (pbk.)
    1. Cookery, Mexican. 2. Low-fat diet—Recipes. I. Title. II. Title: One hundred one great lowfat Mexican dishes. III. Title: One hundred and one great lowfat Mexican dishes.
TX716.M4M375 1995
641.5'638'0972—dc20   95-5282
                                                                         CIP

95 96 97 98 99 AA 10 9 8 7 6 5 4 3 2 1

Printed in the United States of America

A note about nutritional analyses
Food values have been rounded up; trace amounts are listed as zero. Actual figures may vary slightly depending on the brands of food that are used.

How to Order:
Single copies may be ordered from Prima Publishing, P.O. Box 1260, Rocklin, CA 95677; telephone (916) 632-4400. Quantity discounts are available. On your letterhead, include information concerning the intended use of the books and the number of books you wish to purchase.

Contents

Introduction

It is amazing to discover devoted Mexican-food lovers around the world. The passion for spicy, delicious Mexican food continues to grow at an astonishing rate. Nowhere is this more true than in the United States. Americans have an ever increasing infatuation with the virile, flavorful chiles and the spicy sauces of this exotic, brightly colored cuisine. Healthful Mexican-style cookery, prepared with fresh, lean products, provides nutritious dishes that add zest and versatility to enhance your regular daily diet. This cookbook will offer a glimpse of the different types of classical regional cooking found throughout Mexico and the American West and Southwest. These colorful, lowfat dishes have a spicy Mexican style that is great for daily cooking and especially attractive for entertaining guests on formal occasions.

In the United States, the trend for more healthful food has American cooks from coast to coast eagerly searching for lowfat, low-calorie recipes to support simpler, more healthful lifestyles. The idea for this cookbook came from my attempts to adapt my native cuisine and traditional family recipes to leaner, more nutritious recipes. As a result my family and I can eat Mexican dishes as often as we like without worrying about too much fat, sodium, and cholesterol. The wealth of label information and lean food products available in grocery markets today make this a manageable challenge. Upon every visit to the grocery market, you can readily find a newly marketed nonfat or noncholesterol product on the shelf. American food manufacturers have finally caught on and generously offer a growing plethora of lean, low-salt, lowfat, unsweetened or low-cholesterol products. For tortilla lovers, the discovery of one's first package of low-fat flour tortillas is truly an exciting, grateful moment. When the first nonfat avocados become available on the market, I looked forward to a luscious bowl of lowfat guacamole.

With this cookbook, I wanted to help the health-conscious cook learn to create tantalizing, healthful Mexican-style meals. If you are a cook who enjoys living a good lifestyle and wants to avoid unnecessary amounts of calories, sugar, cholesterol, and fat, you will appreciate this cookbook. And if you are a cook who likes to pre-pare spicy, appetizing, attractive foods, you will want to try these appealing recipes. The Mexican style of spicy, exotic cooking blends well with creative innovations to cut fat, sodium, cholesterol, and calories from one's diet. Spicy chiles, sauces, and vegetables are a wonderful way to add zest to an otherwise bland, nutritious diet of fish, lean meats, skinless chicken, or other lowfat or low-cholesterol ingredients. At the end of each recipe, you will find approximate nutritive value information to edu-cate cooks and provide values for suggested servings, including calorie count, grams of protein, fat, and carbo-hydrates, and milligrams of sodium and cholesterol.

I know Mexican cooking fans will agree that it is fun and rewarding to make Mexican cuisine part of one's culinary expertise. These Mexican-style dishes create wonderful flavors which produce a lingering aftertaste that tantalizes your taste buds for several hours. The recipes presented in this cookbook offer a range of spici-ness (for example, 1 to 3 cloves garlic, 2 to 4 sprigs fresh cilantro, or 1/8 to 1 serrano chile) from very mild to very spicy. The level of spiciness for each dish is up to you, the cook in charge. Once you try the recipes, I urge you to adapt the quantity of fresh herbs and chiles according to your personal tastes. If you like spicy foods, use the high end of the range or more. If you like milder foods, use the low end of the range or less.

If you are unacquainted with preparing, cooking, or eating chiles, please read the information about chiles in the Ingredients section (pages 10–21). You will need to understand the intricacies about identifying, selecting, roasting, toasting, steaming, and peeling chiles. Before you can safely, easily, and accurately cook with chiles, you need to know a few things about these intriguing ingredients. Most important, you will want to know what the level of spiciness is for individual chiles. Always remember to use caution when cooking with unfamiliar chiles. Chiles are not always as mild and harmless as they appear.

I know that you will enjoy exploring new ways to adapt these Mexican dishes to suit your tastes and individual living and cooking style. With practice and a little effort, you can enjoy these 101 great lowfat mexican dishes in the comfort of your own kitchen. These are wonderful recipes that you can really enjoy. So will your family and your guests. Happy cooking!

A Brief History of Mexican Cuisine

The Aztec-Mexicas were a powerful tribe of fierce, no-
madic Indians living in central Mexico. The Aztecs ruled
most of the area tribes and created an extraordinary,
highly civilized empire. The jewel of the Aztec empire
was a magnificent city called Tenochtitlán. The Aztec-
Mexicas built Tenochtitlán in the early fourteenth century
on a beautiful lake, surrounded by fertile fields planted
with corn, beans, chiles, and squash. Tenochtitlán was a
city of splendor possessing lavish palaces, temples, and
other elaborate architectural structures. In 1519, Hernán
Cortés, a young Spanish sea captain, arrived on Mexican
shores with six hundred Spanish sailors. Cortés, thrilled
by the riches offered by the Aztec empire, fought two
years to defeat the Aztec Indians. On August 13, 1521,
with their beloved city ravaged by war, the Aztec-
Mexicas surrendered to Cortés.

The Spaniards rebuilt the devastated city of
Tenochtitlán and called it Mexico City. They called the
newly conquered land New Spain and made it part of the
huge Spanish empire. New Spain, later called Mexico,
thus entered a new era of over three hundred years of

Spanish domination. The Spaniards intermarried with the Indians and taught them Christianity. They brought European ideas, customs, and culture to Mexico. Inevitably, they would greatly influence the simple, nutritionally balanced diet of the local Indians. These first Spaniards began the slow process of altering the basic Indian diet, rich in vitamins, protein, and minerals, into what we recognize today as Mexican cuisine. The native Indians were ahead of their time in understanding the intricacies of a nutritious diet. The modest ingredients used by these ancient Indians centuries ago continue to flourish and provide the foundation for today's beloved Mexican dishes.

Mexico is a land offering distinct regional cultures and a festive, fascinating world of exotic tastes, aromas, sights, sounds, and textures. Mexican cuisine reveals the Mexican love of life, family, land, and happiness. Mexicans use brilliant, vivid colors, like luscious reds, shimmering yellows, and cool greens, to express their appreciation of beauty and contrast. You will see the bright colors reflected in their exquisite cuisine through the basic ingredients of corn, chiles, beans, herbs, and tomatoes. Over the past five hundred years, many foreigners came to live in Mexico, including many from Spain, France, the Caribbean, and America. Each culture contributed their culinary skills to influence the evolving Mexican cuisine. The exotic blends of culture over time have created an extraordinary international hybrid cuisine representing many different lands. As a result, traditional dishes differ widely between regions. Interestingly, because of these evolutionary influences over many centuries, like American cuisine, it has become hard to precisely define Mexican cuisine. The real Mexican cuisine is one of variety, vibrant color, and spicy, savory sauces.

Possessing diverse regional climates, long coastlines, and varying topography, Mexico offers an abundance of different types of food products. Crops, such as corn, chiles, vegetables, fruits, and beans, remain the traditional staples of the indigenous Mexican diet. Mexican fishermen have the long coastlines of Mexico, stretching from north to south, to catch the large varieties of fish and shellfish.

You can purchase pork, turkey, chicken, beef, lamb, and eggs in most markets, called *mercados*. Visitors will find gay, lively outdoor markets located in the center or plaza of most cities, small towns, and villages. At these outdoor markets, farmers and vendors offer products in a congenial profusion of commercial and bustling activity. In the larger cities, you will find similar festive markets housed in huge buildings near the downtown area. These indoor markets overflow with vendor stalls jammed awkwardly together along narrow aisles. Vendors offer a variety of enticing products for sale amid the bewitching aromas, curious noises, and brisk activity of busy shoppers. The energetic vendors sell everything imaginable to willing shoppers. In one section, you will discover pyramids of chiles, beans, fruits, and vegetables and large cases filled with meat, poultry, fish, and dairy products. In another area, you will see large piles of clothes, rugs, blankets, and fabrics. Other areas have shelves overflowing with cooking equipment, hardware, pottery, toys, and electronics. The American-style supermarkets in Mexico have a while yet to go before they entirely replace the sociable, energetic fun of shopping at the local *mercado*.

Ingredients

Like Mexico itself, Mexican cuisine is an interesting blend of ancient regional cultures, foreign influences, and an intense love of family and life. The heart of the Mexican family is the kitchen. After centuries of social and cultural change, beans, corn, and chiles remain the traditional foundation of Mexican cuisine. These outwardly ordinary products significantly contribute to an especially nutritious and unique blend of complementary ingredients.

The ingredients used in these recipes represent only a small portion of a vast variety of fascinating food products skillfully used by Mexican cooks. You can find these products in the gay, hectic marketplaces throughout Mexico. In America, you can find most of the basic ingredients at your local grocery market. Today, many local markets maintain a whole section devoted to Mexican ingredients and other related products. If you're lucky, you might even have a Hispanic grocery market in your area where you can find an assortment of chiles, Mexican cheeses, and herbs. Also, many of these ingredients are available through various mail-order catalogs. These catalogs typically provide an assortment of herbs, chiles, salsas, and other related products.

In this cookbook, I adapted many traditional Mexican recipes to fit the cooking styles and ingredients found in the typical American kitchen. These recipes are not elaborate and will not require special cooking equipment, other than a blender, glass baking dish, and Teflon or nonstick skillets, pots, saucepans, and baking sheets. Following, you will find helpful information about storage, preparation, and nutrition for the many ingredients presented in these recipes. If a specialty ingredient is not readily available in your area, you might use an alternative as suggested in this section.

I recommend the use of the freshest, leanest ingredients for flavorful, healthful cooking, including lean meats, lowfat dairy products, and plenty of fresh herbs, chiles, and vegetables. Always choose the freshest, ripest, most unblemished, leanest products to ensure your cooking success. The freshest ingredients add unexpected and flavorful sensations that linger long after you have eaten your meal. Always wash your products in cold water to rid them of chemicals, germs, and dirt. Lastly, remember to always work on clean surfaces. Be especially careful around raw meat. Wash any surface or utensil after it touches raw meat, including poultry, beef, pork, and fish.

Beans, Dried

The simple bean is a deceptively modest vegetable. A rich source of vegetable protein, the remarkable bean is also packed with fiber, minerals, and other valuable nutrients. Beans are surprisingly low in fat and calories. You can healthily substitute dried beans, combined with corn, wheat, rice, or other complementary vegetables and grains, for other types of animal protein, such as meat, chicken, or fish. For centuries, most cultures throughout the world have received their dietary protein from beans and other cheap, nutritious complementary vegetable and grain products. One cup of cooked pinto beans provides 14 grams of protein, .4 grams of fat, and 117 calories.

Throughout North America, approximately twenty-five varieties of dried beans are sold. Dried beans come in different shapes, colors, flavors, and sizes. Popular bean varieties in Mexico are: pinto, black, kidney, pink, and yellow beans. In a large cooking pot, simmer the beans with three to four times as much water until soft. The smaller, less tough beans require one to two hours to cook. The larger, tougher beans require three to four hours. Quickly and with little effort, you can serve a simple, highly nutritious meal of beans served in their own savory broth accompanied by a corn tortilla, tomatoes and chiles. The Indians in Mexico have known this nutrition secret for centuries and continue to rely on this extraordinary combination of vegetable protein.

Beef

Beef is an excellent source of animal protein, vitamins, and minerals. Unfortunately for low-calorie and lowfat diets, meat also contains high amounts of elements, such as saturated fats and cholesterol. Most current medical reports recommend limited use of meat products because of the fat and cholesterol content. Reduce the amount of meat you eat and only buy extra-lean cuts of trimmed meat (without visible marbling and fat) to significantly reduce unhealthful amounts of these elements in your regular diet. Find out about the meats your butcher uses to make his extra-lean ground round meat. Avoid ground round made with meats high in cholesterol and saturated fats. If your grocery store does not already offer extra-lean ground round, here is a solution. Ask the butcher to grind an extra-lean round steak without visible fat and marbling. Make sure the butcher uses a clean grinder without leftover fatty meats stuck between the blades.

Examine the fat content of the extra-lean meats sold in your local grocery store. The leanest meat should not contain more than 15 percent fat. This range of leaness reduces calorie intake, by approximately one-third. Regular meats sold will contribute approximately 30 percent fat or more to your diet, if used. For the leanest cuts of beef, buy round eye or round steak without visible marbling or fat.

Fresh meats are especially perishable and should be kept refrigerated or frozen until they are ready for cooking. To store, refrigerate meat and freeze after twenty-four hours. Be sure to wash all work surfaces that come in contact with raw meat. You can accidentally infect other food ingredients with germs or parasites from the uncooked meat if you work on unclean surfaces or use dirty utensils.

See also *Pork* (page 29).

Cheese

When I travel to a new country, I like to shop at a local market to try the cheeses. Every country has its own varieties of special, unique-tasting cheese. Around the world there are so many wonderful-tasting cheeses and they taste great because they contain lots of fat! Mexico has an equal array of alluring and attractive cheeses that will tempt even the most disciplined palate. Fortunately, you can often find many pleasant-tasting, lowfat cheeses in grocery markets throughout North America. If not, ask your grocery market manager to stock a few varieties. The recipes in this cookbook specify the use of small portions of lowfat cheese to significantly reduce the amount of fat and calories in a dish. Presently, most of the lowfat cheese on the market contains approximately 9 grams of protein, 80 calories, 20 milligrams of cholesterol, and 5 grams of fat per 1 ounce of cheese.

Chicken

See *Poultry* (page 30).

Chiles

Chiles have long played a prominent role in the cuisine of Mexico and many other countries. Since ancient times, chiles continue to enchant the world with their spicy, unique charm. Chiles come in all shapes, sizes, colors, and degrees of spiciness. To the chile novice, trying to figure out the names for the different types of chiles can become very confusing. This task becomes even harder because American companies or grocery markets often mislabel their chiles. To add to the confusion, the names of different chiles vary from region to region.

Two types of chiles are most often available in America: fresh or dried. Each type has varying degrees of spiciness and flavor. Fresh chiles are typically waxy green, red, or yellow in color. Dried chiles, normally red or black in color, wrinkle like dried fruit. Often, you will find dried red chiles used to make powdered or crushed chiles. Chiles are great food ingredients because they have little fat or sodium, few calories, no cholesterol, and fiber and vitamins A and C in abundance. Interestingly, the chile has more vitamin C, by weight, than an orange.

Why are chiles so popular? Most chile lovers say it is because chiles produce tantalizing sensations in the mouth. Others say that chiles add an irresistible aroma to food that tempts our sense of smell. In fact, researchers report that after a regular diet of chiles our taste buds begin to crave the zingy satisfaction created by the indulgent chile. Dried or fresh, chiles create seductive taste sensations that go straight to the brain. Because the brain thinks it is on fire, it hastily secretes endorphins to put out the spicy heat. Endorphins are our body's own pain-killing hormones and create a pleasant feeling or tranquilizing effect. Coincidentally, chiles also create gastric juices that help the body digest food faster and easier.

Many botanists believe that the chile originated in Bolivia, South America, perhaps as long as ten thousand years ago. Later in Peru, Incas used the chile as a healthful food source and curative for ailments like arthritis and the common cold. Often called peppers, chiles spread to Mexican, Asian, and African shores by explorers bringing products from other lands. Today, a quarter of the world's population eats chiles as part of their regular diet. Over the past few centuries, chiles seem to have been slower to ensnare Europe's and America's attention with their spicy, flavorful charm. Today, chiles are enjoying newfound fame and popularity in the West, South, and Southwest states of the United States. Throughout the country, Americans are learning to enjoy the subtle appeal of the spicy chile. For example, many cheesemakers in Wisconsin sell Jack cheese flavored with jalapeño chiles. In the Midwest, many restaurants sell taco salads or tortillas spiced with jalapeño chiles.

Chiles have lots and lots of spicy, tantalizing flavor. *Capsaicin* is the chemical that makes the chile spicy hot. Capsaicin, an odorless and tasteless chemical, concentrates in the seeds, seed oil, and membranes of a chile. The amount of capsaicin varies from chile variety to chile variety. The spiciness of the chile depends on the chemical structure of the capsaicin rather than the amount of the capsaicin in the chile. It's the outer wall of the chile that contains most of the flavor. Wilbur L. Scoville developed the best-known, reliable method to measure a chile's spicy heat. The Scoville Scale measures the level of spiciness in different varieties of chiles. Following is a brief summation of the scale used to measure the approximate spiciness of the most popular Mexican chiles available in the United States:

Scoville units	Type of chile
0	Bell pepper
250–1400	Green or anaheim chile
3000	Poblano chile
3500–4500	Jalapeño chile
4000	Hungarian yellow chile
7000–25,000	Serrano chile
200,000–250,000	Scotch bonnet chile
300,000–350,000	Habanero chile

Wash your hands after handling chiles and their seeds. Rubbing your eyes with chile juice on your fingers can be an especially painful experience. In addition, wear plastic gloves to keep particularly sensitive hands away from chile seeds and juices. If you do burn your finger with chiles, rub your hands with toothpaste to relieve the burning sensation. Chiles are not known to damage the lining of the stomach or intestines, but if you are a first-time chile eater and have chronic stomach problems, please discuss it with your doctor before eating any hot, spicy chiles!

How hot do you like your chiles? There are zealous chile lovers who like to eat the hottest, unseeded chiles whole. Other less zealous chile lovers will need to reduce the spiciness of chiles to a lesser degree of hotness. To do so, carefully remove the seeds and scrape the inside to remove the white fibrous membranes or veins. The seeds contain approximately 20 percent of the spiciness while the veins contain 60 percent. The remaining chile skin contains about 20 percent of the spiciness. With this knowledge, you can attempt to control the spiciness of the chiles added to your meal. It will take a bit of testing but is well worth the effort! Of course, if spicy hot chiles are what you crave, use the whole chile in your next dish — the skin, seeds, and the veins!

Most large grocery stores stock canned chiles in a Mexican or international section. In an emergency, if you cannot find the right chiles in their fresh form, you might substitute canned chiles. However, be aware that canned chiles lose much of their nutritional value through the canning process and contain higher amounts of sodium.

Following is a descriptive list of the many common chiles available in America and presented in this cookbook:

Anaheim Chiles Second
to the jalapeño chile, anaheim chiles are probably the
best-known, most versatile
chiles found in American

grocery markets. Also known as a California or green chile, it is mildly spicy and flavorful. Anaheim chiles are 5 to 7 inches long and 1 to 2 inches wide. Because the waxy, green-colored skin is thick, cooks often roast the chile to peel off the skin. Otherwise, this green chile is

great sautéed or steamed like a bell pepper. Researchers are hard at work to produce a green anaheim chile that has a thin, flavorful skin that cooks will not have to peel. You will find helpful information about peeling chiles in *Roasting and Steaming Chiles* and *Peeling and Seeding Chiles* (page 19).

Chopped, stripped, stuffed, or stewed, the anaheim green chile is a tantalizing ingredient that adds flavor, aroma, spiciness, and color to a variety of Mexican dishes. If you cannot find fresh green anaheim chiles, larger markets often stock canned anaheim chiles in the international or Mexican section. Hopefully, you will always find fresh anaheim chiles available at your local market. The difference in flavor and nutrition between fresh and canned chiles is considerable.

Ancho Chiles   This is one of my favorite chiles. The dried, wrinkled ancho chile is also very popular in Mexico. Its deep, rich flavor is so nutty and pungent it lingers for hours in your 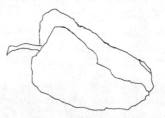 memory. Ancho chiles are actually dried poblano chiles and brownish-red to black in the shape of a small pear. These chiles need to be lightly toasted on a hot skillet then soaked in boiling water for at least an hour to rid them of a mildly bitter aftertaste. Once toasted, this savory chile produces a thick, rich, full-flavored sauce. (See *Toasting Chiles*, page 18, for further helpful information about preparing ancho chiles.) These savory chiles create a prize-winning combination when blended with any of the many special ingredients in the Mexican kitchen.

You can try substituting other dried red chiles, such as pasilla and New Mexico chiles if ancho chiles are unavailable, but there really is not a perfect substitute for the deeply-roasted flavor of the ancho chile. If you do not find ancho chiles available in your market, try drying fresh poblano chiles. (See *Drying Chiles*, page 20, for more about drying poblano chiles.) Otherwise, look for ancho chiles at a Mexican market if you have one in your city. As a last resort, you can substitute 1 tablespoon chili powder for each ancho chile.

Habanero Chiles   If you are in pursuit of a really hot variety of chile, you might like to try the deceptively modest, small habanero chile. The habanero, typically grown in the Yucatán in Mexico, has the distinction of being known as the 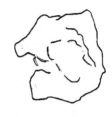 world's hottest chile. It has a capsaicin content of 300,000 to 350,000 Scoville units. Researchers recently tested a variety of the habanero chile called the Red Savina habanero. It is believed to be the world's hottest chile. This chile measures at an incredible 577,000 Scoville units.

   If you want a hotter, spicier dish, you can substitute habanero chiles for the chiles called for in these recipes. *Caution!* Use habanero chiles at your own risk. Habanero chiles will not appear as a required ingredient in any of the recipes in this book. You can sometimes find fresh habanero chiles in the vegetable section of large grocery markets. If you can't find fresh habanero chiles, larger markets often stock canned habanero chiles in the international or Mexican section.

Jalapeño Chiles   Popular in the United States, jalapeños appear on many menu selections throughout the West and Southwest. Originally from the region Jalapa in the state of 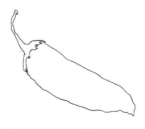 Veracruz, the jalapeño is a small, dark green, plump, waxy chile 2 to 3 inches long and 1 inch wide. New chile eaters will probably find eating an entire jalapeño chile far too potent for their uninitiated palates. Beginners should try the smallest portions at first to slowly adjust to the spicy hotness. Throughout this cookbook, most of the recipes recommend using serrano or jalepeño chiles as an optional ingredient to add spice to each dish. If you find that even the smallest portion of the jalepeño or serrano chile is just too hot for your comfort, you might prefer to omit these chiles from the recipes.

Grocery markets normally stock fresh, green jalapeño chiles in the produce section. Also, your market might stock a variety of pickled or canned jalapeño chiles in their international or Mexican section.

New Mexico Chiles Similar in flavor and appearance to the anaheim green chile, the New Mexico chile is hotter and slightly longer. The fresh New Mexico chile is waxy green and the dried variety is  brownish-red. The New Mexico chile is becoming especially popular for canning and distribution throughout the United States. New Mexicans are proud of the chiles they grow. They have spent many years perfecting the cultivation of the perfect chile. In New Mexico, you will see endless fields of chiles growing in the valley sun. Devoted chile lovers should take the opportunity to travel to these fertile valleys dedicated to the intriguing chile. While there, check out the famous Big Jim chiles that grow up to 12 inches long.

Pasilla Chiles   Like the ancho chile, the dried, wrinkled, black pasilla chile produces an equally intense, savory sauce. This deeply flavored chile is 4 to 6 inches  long and creates an orangish-red sauce that delightfully blends with seafood and noodles. Before using pasilla chiles, lightly toast them in a hot skillet and soak them in boiling water for at least an hour to rid them of an astringent aftertaste. (See *Toasting Chiles*, page 18, for more about preparing pasilla chiles.)

Poblano Chiles   Increasingly popular in the United States, the mild, fresh poblano chile is great for stuffing, roasting, or stripping. Dark green, waxy, and pear-shaped, this large chile is popular for its mildly spicy flavor and color. Poblano chiles are  very similar, in shape and flavor, to bell peppers. If you cannot find poblano chiles in your local market, you might substitute bell peppers. If you can't find them fresh, larger grocery markets often stock canned poblano chiles in the international or Mexican section.

Serrano Chiles   Here is another popular chile. The serrano chile is a small, thin, bright green chile that is hot, flavorful, and extremely versatile. I use this all-purpose chile often in this cookbook because you can reasonably control the spiciness of your dish. If  you like mildly spicy dishes, remove the seeds, finely chop a small portion of the tip and add it to your dish. If you like much spicier dishes, add the whole chile along with the seeds and the veins. Consider the modest, versatile serrano chile as a zesty and healthful way to perk up your meals. If you cannot find serrano chiles in your local market, try substituting the smaller serrano with the less spicy jalapeño chile.

New chile eaters will probably find eating an entire serrano chile far too potent for their uninitiated palates. Beginners should try the smallest portions of this humble-looking chile at first to slowly adjust to the spicy hotness. Throughout this cookbook, most of the recipes recommend using serrano or jalepeño chiles to add spice to each dish. If you find that even the smallest portion of the serrano is just too hot for your comfort, you might prefer to omit these chiles altogether from the recipes.

Grocery markets normally stock fresh green serrano chiles in the produce section, and a variety of pickled or canned serrano chiles may be found in the international or Mexican section.

Chile Powders and Ground Peppers Chile powders and ground peppers are convenient, familiar, and useful if you cannot find the fresh or dried varieties in your local markets. You will normally find chile powders or ground red peppers on the spice shelves of many grocery stores. Use these bottled chile powders and crushed chile peppers as the last resort. Although not fresh or intensely flavorful, powdered or crushed chiles do add spice and blend well with other fresh ingredients. You can make chile powder yourself by grinding toasted, dried red chiles in a blender. One 6- to 7-inch dried red chile creates about 1 tablespoon of red chile powder.

Cleaning Chiles

Rinse fresh or dried chiles in cold water. If you are going to roast chiles, prick them a few times with a fork. These pricks will allow steam to release while you roast the chiles. Once cleaned, you can roast, toast, chop, freeze, dry, or eat the chiles fresh and whole.

Toasting Chiles

Toasting dried chiles softens them and releases the flavors from within the skin. While toasting, sensational aromas will waft through the air in your kitchen. Before toasting the chiles, rinse them in cold water and remove the stems and as many seeds as you like; if you like a less spicy chile, remove all the seeds. Place the chiles in a preheated skillet or griddle over medium-high heat. Frequently turn the chiles over the heat until they puff up with steam and the skin softens. Toast the chiles 5 to 6 minutes. Be careful not to let them burn. Remember to wash your hands after handling chiles.

Roasting and Steaming Chiles

Fresh chiles with thick skins often need their skins roasted and peeled. Roasting gives the chiles a nutty flavor and blisters the skin. Once roasted, you will need to steam the chiles before peeling. Steaming will help loosen the blistered skin from the chile. There are many roasting and steaming methods but in the American kitchen probably the two easiest are as follows:

1. Turn the broiler on. Spread the clean, fresh green chiles on an ungreased baking sheet. Put the baking sheet 2 to 3 inches from the broiler. Broil on each side until the chiles bubble into a blister and slightly brown. With long-handled tongs, turn the chiles to expose and broil any unblemished skin. Once evenly blistered on all sides, place the roasted chiles in a plastic bag. Let the chiles steam in the tightly closed plastic bag for approximately 5 minutes.
2. Hold a chile between long-handled tongs 4 to 5 inches from the flame on a gas stovetop. Slowly rotate the chile over the hot flame until it blisters evenly. To steam chiles, instead of using the plastic bag method, you can wrap the blistered chiles in a damp kitchen towel for 5 minutes. Now the chiles should be ready for peeling. Remember to wash your hands after handling chiles.

Peeling and Seeding Chiles

Once roasted and steamed, peel the blistered skin from the chile under cold water. If the skin does not easily peel off in certain spots, the chile was not thoroughly or evenly roasted; try broiling the chile slightly longer in the unfinished area.

To seed, split one side of the chile from top to bottom and pull out the seeds. Scrape out the seed pod and white membranes or veins of the chile. For some recipes, you will also need to pull or cut off the stem. For stuffed chiles, you might keep the stem in place for decoration. If you like to use dried seeds to create hotter, spicier dishes, save and dry the seeds when you seed the chiles. You can also garnish with dried seeds.

Storing Chiles

To store fresh chiles, refrigerate them in a tightly covered plastic container. Kept refrigerated, they will stay fresh for more than a week. Dried chiles will keep indefinitely if kept in a cool, dark place with ventilation. New Mexicans are famous for storing their dried red chiles tied together to form a long, ornamental strand, called a *ristra*. You can also store green chiles indefinitely in the freezer. Do not freeze the chiles in their fresh state; be sure to roast and steam them first. Tightly seal steamed, unpeeled chiles in a freezer container and place the container in the freezer.

Drying Chiles

Leave green chiles in a cool, dark place with ventilation until the mature chile turns red and loses much of its moisture. Tie three red chiles together by the stems with a long string. Moving upwards an inch, tie five chiles together by the stems along the strand. Continue this process until you have your strand of chiles to the length that pleases you. The strand will look colorful hanging on your kitchen wall in an ornamental *ristra*. Hang your dried chile strand in a dry area with full sunlight and ventilation. For a more elaborate and fuller *ristra*, braid several strands of chiles together.

More About Chiles

If you are a chile enthusiast and would like to know more or keep up with the world of chiles in America, write the Chile Institute in New Mexico:

The Chile Institute
Box 300003, Dept. 3Q NMSU
Las Cruces, NM 88003
(505) 646-3028

The Chile Institute is a nonprofit, international orga-
nization and part of New Mexico State University in Las
Cruces. This group of chile experts devotes their research
efforts to the better understanding, awareness, preserva-
tion, and study of chiles (*Capsicums*).

If you are in New Mexico, take an entertaining visit
to the Chile Institute. The Institute also maintains a Chile
Museum and a Chile Mercado which offers interesting
chile-related information, lore, and products for sale. If
you write or call for information, the Chile Institute will
provide a list of publications for sale to the public. If you
like, you can join the Chile Institute as a member and regularly receive quarterly newsletters and small gifts. The
Chile Institute can also give you information about growing your own hot chiles.

Cilantro

Many ancient cultures hold this simple herb in high
esteem. Cilantro, Chinese parsley, and coriander are a few
of the many names for this charming, aromatic herb. You
can find cilantro in most American grocery markets in the
produce section, tied in small bunches, next to the parsley. Cilantro is the kind of herb that you either learn to
adore or you doggedly avoid. This pungent, delicate herb
has a unique, soapy taste important to Mexican cuisine
and found in many recipes in this cookbook. If you prefer,
you can leave cilantro out of the dish altogether or add it
in the large quantities that you enjoy.

Use every part of the fresh sprigs of cilantro, except
the stems, to enhance the flavor and aroma of your
Mexican dishes. You can also use cilantro as an attractive
fresh, green garnish. This fragile herb, with pretty green
leaves, easily wilts and has a short lifespan. Store cilantro

bunches in the refrigerator with stems immersed in a small bowl of water. Wrap the bowl in a closed plastic bag. The cilantro should stay fresh this way for more than a week.

The bottled and canned versions of dried cilantro, typically called coriander, normally contain the seeds of the cilantro plant, not the familiar green leaves. These seeds do not substitute for the fresh, leafy green tops of the cilantro plant. When cooking with fresh cilantro, wait until the last moment to cut and cook it to release the most aroma and flavor possible; extended cooking reduces the strength. If you want to limit the impact of the cilantro to just a subtle hint of flavor, cook it longer than suggested in these recipes.

Corn

Indians have long considered corn a gift from the gods. More than five thousand years ago, the indigenous Indians of Mexico cultivated and dried corn to make corn flour. They used the corn flour to make the dough for small, round, flat cakes that they heated on a grill and ate with every meal. Today we call these simple corn cakes *tortillas*.

However you prepare this time-honored and nutritious vegetable, use fresh corn to release the sweetest, earthiest flavor. In America, most of the corn eaten today is sweet corn. Always buy and immediately refrigerate corn in its husk to avoid loss of vitamins. To cook corn for use in these recipes, first strip individual corn kernels from the ear with a sharp knife. Grated, fresh corn also makes a tasty garnish for many Mexican dishes.

When you eat corn with beans, these two incomplete, complementary vegetable proteins combine to provide complete protein equal to that of any animal protein. Also, if you combine corn with any animal protein, such as chicken, fish, or eggs, it will contribute to creating complete protein. One-half cup of cooked corn has 2.7 grams of protein, 89 calories, 3 grams of fiber, and 1.1 grams of fat.

Eggs

Fresh eggs are an inexpensive and good source of animal protein. As it is an animal product, eggs also contain large amounts of cholesterol concentrated in the egg yolk. Most researchers agree that we should limit the amount of cholesterol in our daily diets. Fortunately, whole-egg substitutes can replace egg yolks and significantly reduce the quantity of cholesterol. Most of the egg substitutes I've tested consistently retain the flavor and lightness important to most egg dishes. For a good flavor combination, try one whole egg and one egg's worth of whole-egg substitute for every two eggs.

Eggs are especially delicious when combined with tomatoes and chiles. In these recipes, I typically use medium instead of large eggs to limit the amounts of cholesterol and fat. One medium egg provides approximately 6 grams of protein, 70 calories, 190 milligrams of cholesterol, and 4 grams of fat. One whole-egg substitute provides 6 grams of protein, 20 calories, 0 grams of cholesterol, and 0 grams of fat.

Fish

Fish is the real winner over beef, pork, and poultry in the lowfat competition. Many varieties of fish are available throughout North America and cooks have hundreds of wonderful ways to prepare them. Large grocery markets typically offer an appealing variety of fresh fish at an attractive seafood counter. Generally low in fat, fresh, healthy fish are an excellent source of protein, vitamins, and minerals.

Do not store fresh fish in the refrigerator for longer than two days. Before cooking, fish should be at room temperature. To fillet the fish, carefully remove the skin and bones. For great flavor and texture, always cook fish fresh and for as short a time as possible. The short cooking time leaves the succulent flavors in the flesh, without drying it out. Trout, salmon, mackerel, and tuna have a higher fat content than other types of white fish fillets, such as sole, halibut, perch, cod, flounder, and red snapper. The thicker, firmer fish, like trout and salmon, marinate well. This type of fish is excellent grilled, steamed, or poached. The thinner, white fish fillets, do not marinate well. Try broiling or baking these fish on a cooking rack. Avoid anchovies, sardines, caviar, or fish roe as they are high in cholesterol.

Garbanzo Beans

Also known as chickpeas, these nutritious, mild-tasting vegetables provide a valuable source of protein, vitamins, and minerals. Serve garbanzo beans with corn, wheat, rice, or animal protein to provide nutritious, high-protein meals. One-half cup of garbanzo beans provides 7.3 grams of protein, 134 calories, and 2.1 grams of fat.

To clean the garbanzo beans, pick through the beans to remove rocks and cracked or hard beans. Wash the beans and place them in a pot with six to eight cups of boiling water. Heat, let boil for 2 minutes; set aside and cover for one hour. Drain the soaked beans and place them in a large pot with six to eight cups of hot water. Boil gently until the beans become tender.

Garlic

Garlic, like onions and chiles, has been a popular food ingredient for thousands of years. Today, garlic continues to be a great source for iodine, potassium, iron, calcium, sulphur, zinc, nitrogen, magnesium, copper, and vitamins A, B_1, B_2, and C. One clove of garlic provides 4 calories and .2 gram of protein. Health reports suggest that garlic will lower blood pressure, reduce cholesterol, act as a decongestant and fight stomach and colon cancer. Researchers are also examining the ways that garlic can help prevent heart and blood disease. Popular for its curative and restorative powers, garlic has played a significant role in folk medicine around the world for centuries.

To peel garlic, lay an unpeeled clove of garlic flat on a cutting board. Firmly press the flat side of a wide knife down on the clove. The dry, papery skin will separate from the clove of garlic. If you want to coarsely break the garlic while you peel it, rap the wide knife with the bottom of your fist. Cooks have a variety of ways to prepare garlic. If you like, you can mince, chop, roast, powder, crush, or cook garlic whole. Crushing the garlic and cooking it for the shortest amount of time will yield the most aromatic, pungent flavor. To add a roasted, nuttier flavor to your dishes, try cooking with garlic cloves that have been roasted under the broiler. To roast garlic, spread garlic cloves on an ungreased baking sheet and roast them 2 to 3 inches below the broiler until they are lightly browned.

Most of the dishes in this cookbook use cilantro and garlic together. This combination eliminates the garlicky odor from lingering in your mouth after a meal. For garlicky breath, chew on a few sprigs of fresh cilantro or parsley to help reduce the odor until you can brush your teeth. If you have garlicky hands, wash them in salt water to remove the smell of garlic from your fingers.

Always cook with odorless, plump garlic with unblemished, dry, papery skins. Store whole garlic in a brown paper bag in a cool, ventilated place away from the light. Under the right conditions, garlic will keep indefinitely. Store unpeeled cloves of garlic in the refrigerator.

Herbs

Nothing can replace the subtly blended flavor of fresh, whole herbs. Nowadays, to save time and for convenience, our inclination is to use the herbs found in the small containers sold on grocery shelves everywhere. If you do not already, I urge you to try fresh herbs whenever possible. Fresh herbs contribute such a wonderful, earthy difference in flavor. Try a taste test to discover if you can tell the difference between fresh and bottled herbs.

In grocery markets, you can normally find fresh herbs in the produce section. Or you might like to try growing a few of your favorite herbs in small containers on your windowsills. It's fun to watch your herbs slowly grow, day by day. It's also convenient to have them always on hand. In this cookbook, I like to use fresh herbs, such as basil, cilantro, oregano, and thyme to enhance the texture, contrast, and flavor of these Mexican dishes.

Lard

Many traditional Mexican recipes require the use of lard. Lard is fat rendered from meat, most often from pork. In addition, American manufacturers use lard in many store-bought Mexican food items, such as flour and corn tortillas, beans, and tamales. *Caution!* Avoid lard because it has an especially high saturated fat and cholesterol content. Studies show that large amounts of saturated fat might cause or contribute to many health problems, including high blood pressure, high cholesterol levels, clogged arteries, and stroke. Be aware and read food labels to avoid consumption of lard or products made with lard.

Mangoes

The size of a large lemon, this tropical fruit is not well known in the United States. The sweet, delectable mango flesh firmly surrounds a large, hard stone located in the interior of the fruit. Like a peach, cooks must slice the ripe fruit away from the inside stone. Refrigerate this messy, fragile fruit in a tightly sealed plastic container or use immediately. If you cannot find a mango for your recipe, substitute a peach or pear.

Margarine

You might occasionally want to add margarine to the dishes mentioned in this cookbook. In such cases, I recommend the use of lowfat, low-cholesterol margarine. Fortunately, you can find several of these more nutritious margarines stocked in most large grocery markets at a reasonable price. You probably will not notice a great difference in the flavor between regular and lowfat margarine. The big difference is that these leaner margarines significantly reduce the amount of fat, cholesterol, and calories added to your diet. Lowfat, low-cholesterol margarines do have a higher water content that will affect the amount needed for baking. Instead of using margarine, oil, or lard in these recipes, I recommend sautéing, baking, or steaming poultry, meats, and vegetables in their own juices or with small amounts of water.

Meat

See *Beef* (page 9).

Onions, White or Yellow

Onions, uniquely popular in many ancient dishes around the world, are a versatile, flavorful, and time-honored vegetable with highly respected curative powers. Thought to have originated in the Far East, onions have been valued for thousands of years by many cultures.

Onions frequently appear in these recipes because they are an excellent dietary staple, a lowfat source of vitamins and minerals, and appetizing additions to many Mexican dishes. By themselves, onions offer at least 20 percent of the recommended daily allowance of vitamins C and B_6, thiamine, and folic acid. Nutritionists believe that onions provide important natural chemicals to protect the body's heart and circulatory system. Additional research shows that onions can lower blood pressure and can fight against cancer, infection, and diabetes. One-half cup of chopped onion provides .9 gram of protein, 30 calories, and .1 gram of fat.

To add a roasted, nuttier flavor to your dishes, try cooking with roughly chopped, roasted onions. To roast the onions, spread chopped or sliced onions on an ungreased baking sheet and roast them 2 to 3 inches below the broiler until they become lightly browned.

Always select odorless onions with unblemished dry, papery skins. Store onions in a brown paper bag in a cool, ventilated place away from light. With the right storage conditions, onions will keep indefinitely. Remember to store cut or peeled onions in a tightly sealed plastic container in the refrigerator.

Onions, Green

Fresh spring onions, also known as scallions, have a mild flavor. Always select bright green, unblemished stalks. Green onions are healthful ingredients which appear often, raw or cooked, in these recipes. Cut off the root and use the entire onion, including the white bulb and delicate green tops. The green onion creates an attractive, colorful garnish because of its bright green color.

Papayas

This soft, sweet tropical fruit has become more popular in the past few years. The green papaya is a pear-shaped fruit with a mellow, tropical flavor, similar to fresh cantaloupe. About the size of an eggplant, you can seasonally find papayas in the exotic fruit section at a large grocery market. In comparison, the Veracruz papayas sold in Mexico are amazingly huge, about the size of a large watermelon. If you cannot find a papaya for your recipe, substitute cantaloupe or other melon.

To clean a papaya, rinse it under cold water. Use a spoon to clean out the seeds in the center. Once cleaned, you can scoop or cut out the fresh fruit. Use freshly cut papaya immediately or store it in a tightly sealed container in a refrigerator or freezer.

Peppers

See *Chiles* (pages 10–21).

Pineapples

Pineapple, known as the symbol of hospitality, offers a good supply of vitamins and minerals. In addition, pineapples are a valuable aid for the digestion of proteins. Create a decorative pineapple basket by carving out the inside for large fruit and vegetable salads. A pineapple is ripe when it emits a sweet aroma and a dull, hollow sound when rapped with the knuckle. Store pineapples away from sunlight.

To prepare, hold the top of the pineapple and pare the skin with downward strokes away from the fruit until completely skinned. Be sure to remove the dark eyes of the fruit while paring. Once skinned, diagonally slice the pineapple or cut it into wedges. Refrigerate cut pineapple in a tightly sealed container or freeze. One-half cup of fresh, diced pineapple provides .3 gram of protein, 39 calories, 9.6 grams of carbohydrates, and .3 gram of fat.

Pork

Pork, like beef, is a good source of animal protein, vitamins, and minerals—and similarly high in saturated fats and cholesterol. Select and buy the leanest cuts of pork, like tenderloins, without visible marbling and fat. If you eat smaller portions of lean pork, you can meet your daily protein requirements and significantly reduce the amount of cholesterol and saturated fat in your diet.

Most medical reports recommend limited use of pork and other meat products because of their high fat and cholesterol content. Because pork may sometimes, under particular conditions, carry a microscopic parasite, called trichinosis, cooks should always handle pork cautiously and cook the meat thoroughly. You should never serve pork that is rare, medium-rare, or shows any trace of pink meat. Never taste any kind of pork, including sausage, ham, chops, and bacon, in its raw form. Thoroughly clean any cooking utensils and surfaces that touch raw pork before using them again. Slowly cook the meat at least 30 to 45 minutes per pound of pork.

Refrigerate pork in a refrigerator for no longer than one day and freeze after twenty-four hours. You can generally refrigerate larger pieces of meat slightly longer.

Potatoes

Potatoes have an illustrious history and have long provided many cultures a primary food source. Noted as a good source of carbohydrates and fiber, potatoes also provide

3.2 grams of protein per medium-size potato. One-half cup of peeled, diced potato provides 1.6 grams of protein, 59 calories, 13.5 grams carbohydrates and .1 gram of fat.

In recent years, potatoes have suffered from a bad reputation. Fortunately, most of the bad news you read or hear is about what one puts in or on the potato rather than about the nutritious content of the potato itself. Potatoes come in all shapes and sizes; are full of vitamins B and C; and are low in fat, relatively low in calories, and easily digested. Ounce for ounce, potatoes can provide a higher percentage of protein and fewer calories than meat. Always try to use fresh potatoes because processing and drying strip potatoes of their valuable nutrients.

Never cook with blemished or sprouted potatoes. It is best to cook with unpeeled, whole potatoes to conserve valuable nutrients while cooking. Store potatoes in a dry, cool place away from light. Store cooked potatoes in the refrigerator.

Poultry

Poultry is the clear winner over beef in the less fat competition. Versatile, affordable, and quick-cooking, chicken is increasingly popular and an undisputed American and Mexican favorite. Chicken, turkey, and other poultry are excellent sources of protein, vitamins, and minerals. Poultry generally has less cholesterol and saturated fat than beef or pork. A 3-ounce serving of boneless, skinned, cooked chicken breast provides 24 grams of protein, 116 calories, 2 grams of fat, and 72 milligrams of cholesterol. A 3-ounce serving of boneless, skinned, cooked turkey breast provides 26 grams of protein, 119 calories, 1 gram of fat, and 55 milligrams of cholesterol.

Remove the skin and visible fat from poultry before cooking. Also, serve smaller portions to significantly reduce the amount of fat and cholesterol in your diet. Poultry skin contains high amounts of saturated fat. Without the skin, 64 percent of the calories from chicken are from protein and 31 percent of the calories from fat.

Smaller birds are leaner than larger ones. Light meat is leaner, with less fat and cholesterol than dark meat. Also, the breast pieces of poultry are the leanest cuts of chicken. Avoid eating chicken organ parts like hearts, liver, and kidneys because they contain concentrated amounts of cholesterol.

Keep poultry refrigerated or frozen until it is ready to cook. To store, refrigerate poultry and freeze after twenty-four hours. Rinse off all poultry with cold water before cooking. There are many appetizing ways to cook poultry. I offer a few tasty ways to create Mexican dishes with poultry in this cookbook. Sauté, broil, bake, or grill poultry instead of fattier cooking methods, such as roasting or frying. For tastier, tender poultry, brown the pieces in a skillet over medium-high heat to sear in the natural juices and flavor.

Rice

Rice is the world's second most widely harvested grain used for human consumption. Rice, like the potato, is a versatile bargain and also a great side dish for most Mexican-style meals. Americans typically like the long-grain, unconverted white rice. After cooking, the rice should be tender, not soaked or soggy, and each grain should firmly stand apart. Use a fork to easily fluff the rice. If you like your rice more moist and sticky, with a tendency to cling together, use short-grain rice. One absolute cook's tip about cooking rice is: Never stir the rice while it is cooking.

One cup of uncooked, long-grain white rice produces approximately 3 cups of cooked rice. One-half cup of cooked rice provides 2 grams of protein, 100 calories, 22 grams of carbohydrates, and 0 grams of fat. Compared to white rice, brown rice provides 10 more calories per $1/2$ cup of rice and similar amounts of protein, carbohydrates, and fats.

Most nutritionists consider rice an excellent source of complementary protein, especially when eaten with dried peas, beans, wheat, or animal protein. Civilizations throughout time have relied heavily on rice as a staple ingredient for their well-balanced diets of proteins, carbohydrates, fiber, minerals, and vitamins.

Store dried rice in a dry, cool place away from light. Store cooked rice in the refrigerator or freeze after two days.

Shellfish

Versatile, quick-cooking shellfish is increasingly popular for lowfat diets. From country to country, there are many varieties of shellfish. Most large grocery markets offer an enticing variety of fresh shellfish displayed attractively on ice at a seafood counter. Low in saturated fat, fresh, healthful shellfish offers an excellent source of protein, vitamins, and minerals for your healthful diet. Several types of shellfish, such as shrimp, crab, and oysters, are also unfortunately high in cholesterol. These particular shellfish, although low in fat and calories, should be eaten less often and in smaller portions.

Remember to wash shellfish with cold water before using. Store fresh shellfish in the refrigerator and freeze after forty-eight hours. For the most healthful dishes, sauté, broil, bake, boil, or grill shellfish instead of frying it in margarine, oil, or lard.

Spices

See *Herbs* (page 24).

Tomatillos

The small, husk-wrapped, tart-tasting tomatillo, sometimes called a green tomato, is actually a variety of fruit and is most often used as the base for Mexican green sauces. This special fruit enhances the flavor of vegetable, meat, and poultry dishes and shows off the tart, luscious flavor of the distinct-tasting tomatillo. Always buy bright green, unblemished tomatillos while still wrapped in their husks.

To prepare tomatillos, pull off the papery husk, cut out the core, and wash them in cold water. You won't need to peel these spunky little fellows; they have a light, thin skin. To store, refrigerate them in a bowl, but not in plastic bags.

Fresh tomatillos can be found in large grocery markets stocked in the produce section. Also, you might find a variety of pickled or canned tomatillos in the international or Mexican section.

Tomatoes

Tomatoes, known as *tomate* or *jitomate* in Mexico, add a succulent and savory flavor to most Mexican dishes. Probably originally from Peru, tomatoes greatly influenced the indigenous diet of the ancient Indians. Tomatoes continue to greatly influence today's Mexican cuisine, and in the United States, this simple, unsophisticated red treasure is popular with most American cooks. Always select fresh, ripe, round, dark red tomatoes for these dishes. For thicker, more flavorful sauces, use the smaller, pear-shaped tomatoes. In an emergency, you might need to substitute canned tomatoes. However, canned tomatoes lose much of their nutritional value through storing and the cooking process and contain higher amounts of sodium.

The easiest method to peel tomatoes is to place them on an ungreased baking sheet. Roast them 2 to 3 inches from the broiler for 8 to 10 minutes, until the skin turns lightly brown and begins to loosen from the fruit of the tomato. Turn occasionally to broil the entire surface. This method gives the tomatoes a savory roasted flavor. Once the tomato cools, peel the skin off and cut out the core. The second method is to put the tomatoes in a saucepan and cover them in water, then bring the water to a boil and blanch the tomatoes over medium heat. After 8 to 10 minutes the tomato skin should loosen from the pulp. Once the tomato cools, peel the skin off and cut out the core.

Tortillas, Corn

The Spaniards first discovered these delicately browned, round corn cakes, made by the Aztecs, in the sixteenth century. Since ancient times the corn tortilla, a staple food indigenous to Mexico, has endured as a popular ingredient fundamental to many delicious and nutritious Mexican dishes. The corn tortilla is so popular it is found in most large grocery markets in the United States. Today, you can even find *tortillerias*, or tortilla factories, scattered throughout America and Europe.

Corn tortillas vary greatly in thickness, number of calories, and fat content. Search for the freshest, locally made corn tortillas, when possible. Always read the ingredients label and *avoid buying corn tortillas made with lard*. Keep an eye out for fat-reduced corn tortillas which are beginning to appear in grocery stores across America. If you cannot find fresh lowfat tortillas, you might try making your own.

To store, seal corn tortillas in a plastic bag and refrigerate. To warm 1 to 5 corn tortillas, place them in a plastic bag in the microwave oven and heat them for 25 to 60 seconds. To use the oven method preheat the oven to 350°, wrap the corn tortillas in foil and warm for 5 to 10 minutes. Remove the tortillas from the oven and keep them warm wrapped in the foil.

Tortillas, Flour

First there was the corn tortilla and then came the flour tortilla. Flour tortillas are a product of the blended European and Indian cultures after the Spaniards introduced wheat to the Indians. Flour tortillas come in all sizes and thicknesses. Be sure to read the food ingredients label and buy the freshest tortillas that are low in calories and fat and *made without lard*. It was a happy day when I found my first lowfat package of tortillas in the grocery store. If you cannot find lowfat tortillas in your own grocery store, convince your grocery store manager that he needs to stock them for his health-conscious customers.

To store, seal flour tortillas in a plastic bag and refrigerate. To warm 1 to 5 flour tortillas, place them in a plastic bag in a microwave and heat them for 25 to 60 seconds. To use the oven method, preheat the oven to 350°, wrap the tortillas in foil, and warm for 5 to 10 minutes. Remove the tortillas from the oven and keep them warm wrapped in the foil.

Turkey

See *Poultry* (page 30).

Vermicelli

Introduced originally from Italy or Asia by the Spaniards, this thin, spaghetti-like noodle, cooked al dente, blends well with the savory flavors of chiles and tomatoes. Noodles are a good source of protein, carbohydrates, and fiber, especially in combination with vegetables and beans. If you cannot find vermicelli, substitute thin spaghetti noodles.

Vinegars

Vinegars, distilled from wine, have many different flavors and a unique impact on any dish. Known as the oldest fermented liquids, vinegar is probably more than five thousand years old. Most cultures have a variety of uses for vinegar, such as a food ingredient, curative or preventive agent, household cleaner, or preservative. Afficionados often use vinegar to soothe heartburn, varicose veins, asthma, muscle pain, sore throat, burping, sunburn, vomiting, and for pickling vegetables and cleaning windows.

There are many varieties of vinegar. For these recipes, I like to use either apple cider or wine vinegar. Since they are corrosive, be sure not to store vinegars near zinc, aluminum, copper, or iron utensils and pans.

Mexican-style Menus

Preparing festive and colorful Mexican-style meals is easy using the following 22 delicious and attractive selected menus. These menus will help you prepare well-balanced, tasty meals for your family, friends, and special guests. This collection of menus will also help you make your festive, holiday occasions even more sensational. Here is an array of versatile, attractive, easy-to-prepare, delicious meals which are low in fat and only use fresh ingredients. Recipe numbers are next to their titles in the menus. I hope you find a few favorite menus among this selection:

1	*2*
Quick Mexican-Style Breakfast	*Mexican-style Sunday Brunch*
Coffee or Tea	Coffee or Tea
Fresh Orange Juice	Fresh Orange Juice
Sliced Cantaloupe and Melon	Sliced Papaya
Eggs Poached in Ranch Sauce, #24	Rancher's Eggs, #26
Corn Tortillas or Toast	Corn Tortillas or Toast

3
Hearty Mexican-style Luncheon
Fresh Apple Juice
Potato Soup, #10
Soft Chicken Tacos, # 43

4
Light Mexican-style Luncheon
Fresh Apple Juice
Cheese and Chile
Quesadillas, #33

5
Mexican-style Luncheon for Guests
Coffee or Tea
Fresh Pineapple Juice
Seafood Soup, #12
Swiss Enchiladas, #41
Sliced Melon

6
Light Mexican-style Dinner
Coffee or Tea
Chicken Tostadas, #45
Mexican Rice, #52
Fresh Papaya Sauce, #22

7
Mexican-style Picnic
Fresh Lime and Orange Juice
Fresh Fish Appetizer, #90
Taco Salad, #1
Fresh Sliced Papayas

8
Barbecue Grill Menu I
Fresh Pineapple Juice
Tropical Fruit Salad, #6
Zucchini and Corn
Casserole, #56
Grilled Shrimp, #100

9
Barbecue Grill Menu II
Fresh Grapefruit Juice
Tropical Fruit Salad, #6
Spicy Pinto Beans, #64
Grilled Chicken, #84

10
Festive Sports Game Get-Together
Coffee or Tea
Meat with Chile, #74
French Bread or Roll
Sliced Kiwis and Bananas

11
Veracuz Dinner
Fresh Pineapple Juice
Veracruz Salad, #3
Spicy Vermicelli, #51
Red Snapper Veracruz, #92

12
Elegant Dinner for Guests
Coffee or Tea
Fresh Fish Appetizer, #90
Tomatillo and Tomato
Salad, #7
Mexican Green Rice, #57
Salmon Steaks in Green
Chile Sauce, #99
Fresh Papaya Sauce, #22

13
Sunday Family-style Dinner
Coffee or Tea
Mexican Rice, #52
Spicy Green Beans and
Mushrooms, #68
Mexican Meat Loaf, #70
Sliced Mandarin Oranges

14
Quick Sunday Family-style Dinner
Coffee or Tea
Spinach Salad, #5
Meatball Soup, #11
French Bread or Roll
Sliced Papayas and Bananas

15
Quick Mexican-style Dinner
Coffee or Tea
Pinto Beans, #63
Beef in Red Chile Sauce, #77
Corn Tortillas

16
Festive Holiday Meal
Shrimp Salad, #2
Spicy Pinto Beans, #64
Corn with Chile Strips, #54
Sea Scallops in Spicy Red
Sauce, #93
Sliced Papayas and Bananas

17
Mexican Fiesta
Chicken Soup with Tortilla
Strips, #13
Mexican Rice, #52
Green Enchiladas with
Chicken, #36
Fresh Papaya Sauce, #22

18
Quick Seafood Dinner
Lime Marinated Tomato
Slices
Spicy Vermicelli, #51
Mexican Seafood Creole, #97
Fresh Papaya Balls and
Banana Slices

19
Seafood Dinner
Shrimp Salad, #2
Spicy Garbanzos, #55
Baked Fish in White
Wine Sauce, #96
Sliced Oranges with
Lime Juice

20
South-of-the-Border Steak Dinner
Tossed Salad
Pinto Beans, #63
Spicy Mexican-style
Steak, #79
Sliced Melon and Bananas

21
Chicken Dinner
Chicken Salad, #4
Southwestern Vegetable
Medley, #60
Pineapple Chicken, #89
Sliced Melon and Bananas

22
Festive Fajita Dinner
Tossed Salad
Mexican Green Rice , #57
Grilled Chicken Strips, #85
Pineapple Slices and Bananas

Mexican Salads and Soups

Though not indispensable, salads and soups are a welcome addition to any Mexican meal. Soups and salads add bright colors, zesty flavors, and contrasting texture to enhance ordinary fare. Open-air markets in Mexico overflow with familiar and unfamiliar products stocked high in festive market stalls. Such colorful products will entice even the most determined and demanding shopper looking for those special ingredients for hearty soups and garden-fresh salads. You will find most of these same or similar fresh products stocked in your own favorite local market. Fresh, ripe, red tomatoes, piquant chiles, green and white onions, rice, beans, and small bunches of fresh sprigs of cilantro are pleasing additions to any soup or salad and especially favorable in price. If you are a health-conscious cook, you will enjoy adding these savory, aromatic soups and fresh salads to your repertoire of fine, classic dishes. These recipes feature a unique collection of nutritious, delicious dishes to serve your family, friends, and special guests. *Mexican Salads and Soups* includes an appealing assortment of light, healthful, and tasty soups and salads for you to try. These soups and salads can make meals in themselves or complement your dinner as a first course or starter dish.

Traditional salads in Mexico are often different from typical American salads. Most Mexican salads, except for the traditional holiday salads, are simple, fresh combinations of lettuce, tomatoes, or cooked vegetables served as garnish for a delectable meal. The recipes included in this section feature mostly Americanized salad dishes that present delectable, low-calorie salads as a light main course for lunch, a side dish, or a late-night snack. These luscious, attractive salads will subtly reveal the exotic essence of Mexican cookery.

Good soup is an important part of many satisfying, fulfilling meal. The Mexican soups presented in this section are special, homespun, nutritious meals displaying a colorful array of piquant, enticing flavors and interesting textures. A hot, steaming bowl of spicy, fragrant soup is heavenly on a cold afternoon or as an appetizing starter for an elegant meal. In a cup or small bowl, you will also appreciate these thick, savory soups as a late-night snack. If you feel a little under the weather, you can rest better with a cup of nourishing soup to soothe away your illness. These quick, easy-to-prepare, versatile recipes will stimulate the senses, warm and soothe the body, or set the stage for the delicious meal to follow.

Here are a few tips for cooking the perfect soups and salads that your family and friends will rave about. Keep the rest of the meal in mind when you plan your soup or salad. As side dishes, soups and salads, should be nutritious and stimulate the appetite for the meal to come. Always use fresh fruit and vegetable ingredients and wash them thoroughly in cold water before using. Leftovers are a great addition for sparking new life in soups and salads. You can make soups in advance and easily store them in the refrigerator or freezer. Use garnishes like tomato, lime or lemon wedges, a sprig of cilantro, or chopped green onions to dress up soups and salads. Make every soup or salad a brilliantly colored, visual feast of flavor.

Mexican Salads and Soups

1

Taco Salad
(Ensalada de Carne)

Preparation time: 25 minutes
Cooking time: 10 minutes
Preheat oven to 350°

Taco salads always appear as an exceptionally festive and enticing feast of colorful ingredients. Served with a heap of shredded lettuce and tomatoes, this healthful, hearty salad has become popular as an appetizing lunch or dinner. Now you can prepare this attractive, low-calorie salad in a tortilla basket in the convenience of your own home. This recipe serves two large salads. If you prefer, you can use 6-inch flour tortillas to make salad baskets for four smaller salads. This salad is also a great way to use leftover poultry, fish, or beef.

2 fresh lowfat flour tortillas (10-inch)
¼ pound extra-lean ground round
¼ cup red onions, finely chopped
1 to 2 cloves garlic, crushed in a garlic press
⅓ cup Red Chile Sauce (Recipe #16)
2 tablespoons lime juice
1 tablespoon apple cider vinegar
⅛ to 1 fresh serrano or jalapeño chile, seeded, washed, and finely chopped (optional, for a spicier dish)
2 sprigs fresh cilantro, minced (optional)
2 cups iceberg lettuce, shredded
½ cup red bell peppers, halved, seeded, and cut into thin strips

1 small ripe tomato, diced
1/3 cup green onions, finely sliced
salt and freshly ground pepper

Wrap the flour tortillas in foil. Warm the tortillas in preheated oven for 5 minutes until the tortillas are soft. Sauté the meat, red onion, and garlic in a skillet over medium heat until the meat cooks thoroughly and the onions become tender; set the meat mixture aside to cool.

To make the dressing, combine the Red Chile Sauce, lime juice, apple cider vinegar, chile, and cilantro in a jar with a tight-fitting lid. Cover and shake the jar to blend the dressing thoroughly; refrigerate.

To make the two flour tortilla baskets or taco shells, cut two 11-inch circles from heavy-duty foil. Shape each piece of foil into a wide, ruffled basket. Place each warm flour tortilla in a foil basket; shape tortilla to fit the foil shape of the basket. Set the baskets on an ungreased baking sheet. Bake the baskets in preheated oven for 5 minutes; cool the baskets.

Attractively layer one-half portion of the lettuce, meat mixture, and red bell peppers to fill each taco shell. Top each salad with the diced tomatoes and green onions. Pour the dressing over the top of salad. Salt and pepper the salad according to individual taste.

Serves 2

Each serving provides:

157	Calories	4 g	Carbohydrate
7 g	Protein	20 mg	Sodium
1 g	Fat	13 mg	Cholesterol

2

Shrimp Salad
(Ensalada de Camarón)

Preparation time: 15 minutes

Shrimp lovers will satisfy their insatiable desire for
shrimp with this large, succulent, tangy salad. Try substituting squid or octopus for the shrimp to create an attractive variation of this garden-fresh salad. Served with a
slice of toasted bread and cottage cheese, this exotic salad
provides a very attractive, tempting lunch.

$^1/_2$ pound raw medium-size shrimp, peeled and
    deveined
3 tablespoons lime juice
1 tablespoon apple cider vinegar
1 tablespoon cold water
1 teaspoon fresh thyme, minced
1 teaspoon fresh basil, minced
$^1/_4$ cup red onions, finely sliced
$^1/_2$ cup celery, finely sliced
1 cup fresh snow peas, steamed
$^1/_2$ cup red bell peppers, seeded, washed,
    and finely chopped
$^1/_2$ cup yellow bell peppers, seeded, washed,
    and finely chopped
$^1/_8$ to 1 fresh serrano or jalapeño chile, seeded,
    washed, and finely chopped (optional, for
    a spicier dish)
1 bunch spinach (about 3 cups),
    cleaned and torn
1 small ripe tomato, cut into 6 wedges

½ cup green onions, finely sliced
2 to 4 sprigs fresh cilantro, minced
salt and freshly ground pepper

In a saucepan, bring 2 cups of water to a boil. Add shrimp
to boiling water (the water should barely cover the
shrimp); reduce heat. Simmer shrimp for 4 minutes until
the shrimp turns pink. Drain and cool under cold water;
set aside.

Combine the lime juice, apple cider vinegar, cold
water, thyme and basil in a large bowl; mix well. Stir in
the shrimp and remaining ingredients, excluding the
spinach, tomato, green onions, and cilantro.

Place the spinach on six individual salad plates.
Arrange one-sixth portion of the shrimp mixture on top of
each plate. Attractively arrange the tomato wedges to the
side of the shrimp mixture. Garnish each salad with fresh
green onions and minced cilantro. Salt and pepper the
salads according to individual taste.

Serves 6

Each serving provides:

111	Calories	7 g	Carbohydrate
19 g	Protein	74 mg	Sodium
1 g	Fat	35 mg	Cholesterol

3

—✥—

Veracruz Salad

(Ensalada Veracruzana)

Preparation time: 15 minutes
Refrigeration time: 15 to 30 minutes

This attractive, refreshing salad recalls the delicious, fresh
flavors of the open vegetable and fish markets of Veracruz.
Any small, white fish marinated in lime juice will work
well with this colorful salad. For an interesting variation,
add tender, cooked flowerets of broccoli or cauliflower. To
complement this salad for a complete lunch, serve this
appetizing salad with a dab of cottage cheese.

1 cup fresh tuna, cooked, cut into 1-inch pieces
3 tablespoons lime juice
2 sprigs fresh cilantro, minced
$1/2$ cup green bell peppers, seeded, washed, and
    finely chopped
$1/2$ cup red bell peppers, seeded, washed, and
    finely chopped
1 cup mushrooms, thinly sliced
$1/2$ cup celery, finely sliced
1 teaspoon fresh oregano, minced
1 teaspoon fresh thyme, minced
1 bunch spinach (about 3 cups), cleaned
    and torn
1 medium ripe tomato, cut into 12 wedges
1 small cucumber, cut into 12 slices
1 tablespoon apple cider vinegar
$1/2$ cup green onions, finely sliced
salt and freshly ground pepper

Place the tuna and 2 tablespoons of the lime juice in an ungreased, rectangular, glass baking dish. Rub the tuna in the marinade to coat the tuna with the lime marinade. Refrigerate in the marinade for 15 to 30 minutes; drain.

Toss remaining ingredients together in a medium-size bowl, excluding the tuna, spinach leaves, tomato, cucumber, apple cider vinegar, green onions, and remaining 1 tablespoon of lime juice. Stir in the tuna and 1 cup of the spinach leaves.

Place the remaining spinach leaves on six salad plates. Arrange one-sixth portion of the tuna salad mixture on each plate. Attractively arrange 2 tomato wedges and 2 cucumber slices on the side of each salad. Mix the remaining lime juice and apple cider vinegar together in a small glass. Sprinkle each salad with the juice mixture. Garnish the top of each salad with fresh green onions. Salt and pepper the dish according to individual taste. Serve the salad cold.

Serves 6

Each serving provides:

71	Calories	7 g	Carbohydrate
10 g	Protein	61 mg	Sodium
1 g	Fat	18 mg	Cholesterol

4

Chicken Salad
(Ensalada de Pollo)

Preparation time: 15 minutes

The blended, refreshing juices in this large, festive chicken salad highlight the contrasting, scintillating flavors of limes and pineapples. You can substitute turkey or grilled chicken to create another tasty version of this attractive, mouth-watering salad. This salad is a perfect light luncheon or starter dish for dinner. To complement a complete meal, split this recipe in half to serve smaller dinner salads.

½ cup green onions, finely sliced
1 cup chicken, cooked and cut into small chunks
½ cup pineapple, cut into small chunks
½ cup pineapple juice
1 cup small mushroom caps, sliced in half
½ cup garbanzo beans, cooked
½ cup red bell peppers, washed, seeded, and
    finely sliced into 2-inch pieces
½ cup yellow bell peppers, washed, seeded, and
    finely sliced into 2-inch pieces
1 bunch spinach (about 3 cups), cleaned
    and torn
1 small ripe tomato, halved and cut into 12 slices
3 tablespoons lime juice
salt and freshly ground pepper

Combine all the ingredients, excluding the spinach, lime juice, and tomato, in a medium-size bowl; mix well. Salt and pepper the salad according to individual taste. Place the spinach in equal portions on six small plates. Drain the chicken mixture; reserve the marinade. Arrange the chicken mixture atop the spinach on each plate. Garnish each salad plate with the tomato slices. Sprinkle the lime juice and remaining marinade over each salad. Serve the salad cold.

Serves 6

Each serving provides:

105	Calories	21 g	Carbohydrate
17 g	Protein	67 mg	Sodium
2 g	Fat	32 mg	Cholesterol

5

Spinach Salad
(Ensalada de Espinaca)

Preparation time: 15 minutes

Garbanzo beans provide plenty of protein for this spinach
salad topped with a tangy green chile salad dressing.
Serve this light, refreshing salad before dinner or as a
late-night snack. For a satisfying, one-dish lunch packed
with protein, add crackers and cottage cheese.

1 small bunch spinach (about 3 cups), cleaned
    and torn
⅓ cup red onions, halved and finely sliced
1 cup mushrooms, sliced
1 cup garbanzo beans, cooked
1 cup red bell peppers, washed, seeded, and diced
1 cup yellow bell peppers, washed, seeded,
    and diced
⅓ cup Green Chile Sauce (Recipe #15)
2 sprigs fresh cilantro, minced
2 tablespoons apple cider vinegar
2 tablespoons lime juice
1 small ripe tomato, cut into 12 wedges
1 small cucumber, cut into 12 slices
½ cup green onions, finely sliced
salt and freshly ground pepper

Combine all the ingredients, excluding the tomato,
cucumber, and green onions, in a medium-size bowl; mix
well to coat the spinach leaves with the marinade. Place
equal portions of the spinach salad mixture on six salad

plates. Arrange the tomato wedges and cucumber slices on the side of each salad. Garnish the top of each salad with the fresh green onions. Salt and pepper the dish according to individual taste.

Serves 6

Each serving provides:

82	Calories	16 g	Carbohydrate
5 g	Protein	48 mg	Sodium
1 g	Fat	0 mg	Cholesterol

6

—⁂—

Tropical Fruit Salad

(Ensalada de Fruta)

Preparation time: 15 minutes
Refrigeration time: 10 minutes

Fruits, in all shapes, sizes, and colors, are very popular
and widely available throughout Mexico. Fruit lovers will
enjoy the sweet, ripe flavors of the exotic fruits found in
this festive yet simple fruit salad. This kind of salad is
especially pleasing before a spicy Mexican-style meal.

¹/₄ cup lime juice
¹/₂ cup pineapple juice
¹/₂ cup banana, sliced
1 cup mango, cut into 1-inch pieces
1 cup fresh pineapple, cut into 1-inch pieces
2 cups papaya, cut into 1-inch pieces
1 orange or tangerine, peeled and sectioned
3 sprigs mint leaves, minced (optional)
1 bunch spinach leaves (2 cups), cleaned and torn

Combine all the ingredients, excluding the spinach leaves,
in a medium-size bowl; mix well. Cover; refrigerate the
salad for 10 minutes. Drain the fruit marinade; reserve
the marinade. Arrange the spinach leaves on six salad
plates. Decoratively arrange one-sixth portion of the fruit

salad on each salad plate covered with spinach leaves.
Drizzle the remaining marinade over individual salads.
Serve the salads cold.

Serves 6

Each serving provides:

97	Calories	27 g	Carbohydrate
2 g	Protein	19 mg	Sodium
1 g	Fat	0 mg	Cholesterol

7

— ❧ —

Tomatillo and Tomato Salad

(Ensalada de Tomatillo)

Preparation time: 15 minutes

The small, husk-wrapped, tart-tasting tomatillo is actually a variety of fruit and most often used as the base for an exotic green sauce. This recipe enhances the flavors of the vegetables and shows off the tart flavor of the distinct-tasting tomatillo. Garden-fresh, ripe tomatoes and tomatillos are a luscious treat when combined with the tangy flavor of lime juice.

3 medium tomatillos, husked and thinly sliced
2 small ripe tomatoes, halved and sliced
$1/2$ cup green onions, finely sliced
$1/2$ small cucumber, quartered and finely sliced
$1/2$ cup yellow bell peppers, seeded, washed, and
    finely sliced
2 sprigs fresh cilantro, minced (optional)
3 tablespoons Green Chile Sauce (Recipe #15)
2 tablespoons apple cider vinegar
4 tablespoons lime juice
1 teaspoon fresh thyme, minced
1 bunch spinach (about 3 cups), cleaned
    and torn
salt and freshly ground pepper

Combine all the ingredients, excluding the spinach, in a large bowl. Toss the ingredients in the bowl to coat them with the marinade. Add the spinach; mix well. Arrange one-sixth portion of the salad mixture on six salad plates. Salt and pepper the dish according to individual taste.

Serves 6

Each serving provides:

33	Calories	7 g	Carbohydrate
2 g	Protein	39 mg	Sodium
1 g	Fat	0 mg	Cholesterol

8

—⁂—

Spicy Split Pea Soup
(Sopa de Chícharo Pelado)

Preparation time: 15 minutes
Cooking time: 1 to 1¹/₂ hours

This savory, high-protein soup will get your attention.
Full of slowly simmered, flavorful, dried split peas and
chiles, you can serve this nourishing soup to your family
or friends with pride. If you like a smoother soup, purée
the cooked peas in a blender. This soup is a great starter
for a full, nutritious meal. For a hearty lunch or light dinner, serve this tempting soup with a fresh garden salad
and toast.

³/₈ pound (⁷/₈ cup) dried green split peas
9 cups water
2 cups low-salt broth
2 fresh anaheim chiles, seeded, washed, and
       finely chopped
¹/₈ to 1 fresh serrano or jalapeño chile, seeded,
       washed, and finely chopped (optional, for a
       spicier dish)
1 medium white onion, finely sliced
¹/₂ cup green onions, finely sliced
1 to 2 cloves garlic, crushed in a garlic press
1 cup celery, finely sliced
¹/₂ carrot, finely sliced
1 teaspoon fresh oregano, minced
2 bay leaves
salt and freshly ground pepper

Rinse the dried peas in cold water. Place the dried split peas in a large pot with the remaining ingredients. Cover; bring the soup to a boil; reduce the heat to medium-low.

Simmer the soup for 1 to 1½ hours until the peas become tender, according to individual taste. Remove bay leaves. Coarsely smash the peas with a spoon. Serve the hot pea soup immediately.

Serves 6

Each serving provides:

150	Calories	5 g	Carbohydrate
2 g	Protein	8 mg	Sodium
0 g	Fat	0 mg	Cholesterol

9

❧

Mexican-style Tomato Soup

(Sopa de Jitomate)

Preparation time: 15 minutes
Cooking time: 20 minutes

If you have ever wanted to enhance the flavor and texture
of tomato soup, this is a sophisticated version of a well-
known Mexican and American soup. Simmered with the
flavor of tomatoes, chiles, and cilantro, this zesty soup is
equally appealing to the eye and to the taste buds.

1 fresh anaheim chile
8 sprigs fresh cilantro
1 medium white onion, finely sliced
1/2 cup green onions, finely sliced
1 to 2 cloves garlic, crushed in a garlic press
1/8 to 1 fresh serrano or jalapeño chile, seeded,
        washed, and finely chopped (optional, for a
        spicier dish)
1/2 cup bell peppers, seeded, washed, and diced
6 medium ripe tomatoes, blanched or roasted,
        peeled, seeded, and finely chopped
2 cups Mexican Tomato Sauce (Recipe #17)
1/4 cup long-grain rice, uncooked
3 cups low-salt broth
5 cups water
1 teaspoon fresh thyme, minced
salt and freshly ground pepper

Preheat the broiler. Roast the anaheim chile 2 to 3 inches
under the broiler for 3 to 4 minutes on each side.

Occasionally rotate the chile until it evenly browns and blisters on each side. Put the chile in a tightly closed plastic bag to steam for 5 minutes. Carefully peel off the charred skin. Cut off the stem, seed, rinse, and finely chop; set aside.

Mince 2 sprigs cilantro. Sauté the white and green onions, garlic, serrano chiles, and bell peppers with 2 tablespoons of water in a large pot over medium-high heat until the onions become tender; stir frequently. Add the tomatoes and cook 2 minutes; reduce heat to low.

Purée ½ portion of the sautéed tomato and onion mixture in a blender. Return purée to soup pot. Stir in the remaining ingredients, excluding cilantro; combine thoroughly. Add 2 sprigs minced cilantro. Cover; simmer the tomato soup for 20 minutes until the rice is tender. Salt and pepper the dish according to individual taste. Serve the soup in bowls garnished with the remaining fresh cilantro sprigs.

Serves 7

Each serving provides:			
84	Calories	19 g	Carbohydrate
3 g	Protein	26 mg	Sodium
1 g	Fat	0 mg	Cholesterol

10

—❧—

Potato Soup
(Sopa de Papas)

Preparation time: 15 minutes
Cooking time: 20 to 25 minutes

Potatoes come in all shapes and sizes and are packed with
vitamins B and C, minerals, and protein. This soup presents the specially blended flavors of chiles, tomatoes, and
potatoes to perfection. Nutritious, thick, and filling, this
soup offers a satisfying flavor and favored meal to lovers
of hearty soups. For an interesting variation, substitute
the potatoes and carrots with red beans and rice.

1 medium white onion, finely sliced
¹/₂ cup green onions, finely sliced
1 to 2 cloves garlic, crushed in a garlic press
2 fresh anaheim chiles, seeded, washed, and
    finely chopped
¹/₈ to 1 fresh serrano or jalapeño chile, seeded,
    washed, and finely chopped (optional, for
    a spicier dish)
1 cup celery, finely sliced
1 medium ripe tomato, blanched or roasted, peeled,
    and finely chopped
1 medium carrot, pared and thinly sliced
3 cups russet potatoes, pared and diced
2 cups low-salt chicken broth
5 cups water
1 teaspoon fresh oregano, minced
1 bay leaf

1 teaspoon fresh thyme, minced
2 to 4 sprigs fresh cilantro, minced (optional)
salt and freshly ground pepper

Sauté the white and green onions, garlic, anaheim and
serrano chiles, and celery with 2 tablespoons of water in a
large, 5- to 8-quart saucepan over medium-high heat until
the onions become tender; stir frequently. Add the tomato, carrot, and potatoes to the pot; cook 3 minutes, stirring often. Stir in the remaining ingredients, excluding
the cilantro. Cover; bring the mixture to boil over high
heat; reduce heat to low. Simmer soup 20 to 25 minutes
until potatoes become tender. Salt and pepper the soup
according to individual taste. Remove bay leaf. Serve the
hot soup in bowls immediately. Garnish each bowl with
the fresh minced cilantro.

Serves 6

Each serving provides:

97	Calories	22 g	Carbohydrate
3 g	Protein	38 mg	Sodium
1 g	Fat	0 mg	Cholesterol

11

❦

Meatball Soup
(Sopa de Albóndigas)

Preparation time: 15 minutes
Cooking time: 1 hour

Popular throughout Mexico, this savory and nourishing meatball soup is a fabulous blend of rich flavors. The tantalizing flavors of the meat and tomatoes simmer together to make a mouth-watering, one-dish meal. This traditional specialty is also a family favorite. Quick and easy to prepare, you will especially love this delicious, filling soup for supper on a cold, rainy day. To reduce fat and cholesterol, try substituting the fresh egg with a whole-egg substitute.

³/₄ pound extra-lean ground round
¹/₄ cup long-grain rice, uncooked
1 egg
1 medium white onion, finely sliced
1 to 2 cloves garlic, minced
¹/₈ to 1 fresh serrano or jalapeño chile, seeded,
        washed, and finely chopped (optional, for
        a spicier dish)
1 fresh anaheim chile, seeded, washed, and finely
        chopped (optional, for a spicier dish)
4 medium ripe tomatoes, blanched or roasted,
        peeled, and finely chopped
2 cups low-salt beef broth
7 cups water
1 teaspoon fresh oregano, minced

1 teaspoon fresh thyme, minced
2 bay leaves
salt and freshly ground pepper

Combine meat, rice, and egg in a small bowl. Roll meat mixture into 1½-inch balls; set aside. Sauté the onions, garlic, and serrano and anaheim chiles over medium-high heat with 2 tablespoons of water in a 5-quart pot until the onions become tender; stir frequently. Add the tomatoes and cook for 2 minutes. Stir in remaining ingredients, excluding meatballs. Bring the soup to a boil and gently drop the meatballs in the pot. Cover; simmer 1 hour. Skim off excess fat before serving and remove bay leaves. Salt and pepper according to individual taste. Serve the hot soup in bowls immediately.

Serves 6

Each serving provides:

171	Calories	14 g	Carbohydrate
20 g	Protein	61 mg	Sodium
4 g	Fat	71 mg	Cholesterol

12

—❧—

Seafood Soup

(*Sopa de Mariscos*)

Preparation time: 20 minutes
Cooking time: 30 minutes

The simmered flavors of these fruits of the sea give life to
a very delicious, appealing soup. You can vary this recipe
with a different assortment of seafood, including a variety
of firm white fish, squid, and octopus. Serve this soup
with a wedge of lime on the side for extra flavor.

8 sprigs fresh cilantro, minced (optional)
1 medium white onion, quartered and finely sliced
¹/₂ cup green onions, finely sliced
1 to 3 cloves garlic, minced
1 cup celery, finely sliced
1 fresh anaheim chile, seeded, washed, and
    finely chopped
1 medium ripe tomato, finely chopped
¹/₃ cup assorted white fish, boned, skinned, and cut
    into 1¹/₂-inch cubes
¹/₃ cup assorted seafood (scallops, clams, mussels)
2 tablespoons lime juice
4 cups water
2 cups low-salt broth
1 cup Red Chile Sauce (Recipe #16)
1 teaspoon fresh thyme, minced
1 bay leaf
1 teaspoon fresh oregano, minced
salt and freshly ground pepper

Mince 2 sprigs of cilantro. Sauté the white and green onions, garlic, celery, and anaheim chiles over medium-high heat with 2 tablespoons of water in a 5-quart pot until onions become tender; stir frequently. Stir in the tomato, white fish, and assorted seafood; cook 3 minutes. Add the 2 sprigs minced cilantro and remaining ingredients. Bring soup to a boil; reduce heat to low. Cover; simmer gently for 30 minutes until the fish pulls apart with a fork. Remove the bay leaf. Salt and pepper the dish according to individual taste. Serve the hot soup in bowls garnished with the remaining fresh cilantro sprigs.

Serves 6

Each serving provides:

76	Calories	8 g	Carbohydrate
9 g	Protein	73 mg	Sodium
1 g	Fat	18 mg	Cholesterol

13

❧

Chicken Soup with Tortilla Strips
(Sopa de Pollo con Tortillas)

Preparation time: 30 minutes
Cooking time: 10 minutes

Popular throughout Mexico, this is a zesty chicken soup that is homemade in taste, hearty, delicious, and very nutritious. The chicken, herbs, and vegetables present a pleasing contrast of appealing textures, colors, and flavors. This classic Mexican soup will quickly become one of your favorite treats. Simple and very easy to prepare, try this simple soup recipe for a light but filling lunch or dinner.

1 fresh anaheim chile
3 medium ripe tomatoes, blanched or roasted,
    peeled and cut into small wedges
1 to 2 cloves garlic, chopped
1½ cups extra-lean chicken, skinned, boned, and
    coarsely chopped
1 small white onion, quartered and finely sliced
½ cup green onions, finely sliced
1 cup celery, sliced
6 cups water
2½ cups low-salt broth
1 teaspoon fresh oregano, minced
1 teaspoon fresh thyme, minced
1 fresh lowfat flour tortilla (6-inch)
1 to 3 sprigs fresh cilantro, minced
salt and freshly ground pepper

Preheat the broiler. Roast the anaheim chile 2 to 3 inches under the broiler for 3 to 4 minutes on each side. Occasionally rotate the chile until it evenly browns and blisters on each side. Put the chile in a tightly closed plastic bag to steam for 5 minutes. Carefully peel off the charred skin. Cut off the stem, seed, rinse, and finely chop the chile; set aside.

Purée the tomatoes, garlic, and anaheim chile in blender; set aside. Brown the chicken over medium-high heat in a 5-quart pot to sear in the juices; turn frequently. Add the white and green onions and celery; sauté the mixture until onions become tender. Stir in water and broth. Cover; bring to boil over high heat; reduce heat to medium-low. Add tomato purée, oregano, and thyme; mix well. Cover; cook 10 minutes over low heat. Salt and pepper the soup according to individual taste.

Cut the flour tortilla in half then cut further into ½-inch-wide strips. Spread tortilla strips evenly across a large baking sheet. Warm in preheated oven at 300° for 5 minutes. Serve the soup piping hot from a tureen garnished with the tortilla strips and fresh minced cilantro.

Serves 6

Each serving provides:

123	Calories	10 g	Carbohydrate
18 g	Protein	78 mg	Sodium
2 g	Fat	48 mg	Cholesterol

Mexican Sauces

Sauces, called *salsas* in Spanish, are fundamental to the Mexican diet. Salsas reveal the true essence of classical Mexican cuisine. Refreshing, tingly, rich, spicy, mouthwatering, and magical, these flavorful, versatile Mexican sauces proudly proclaim their unique, exquisite delicacy. The spicy, rich taste of a red chile sauce, the subtle flavor of a green chile sauce, or the light, cool freshness of a tropical fruit sauce offer enthusiastic cooks an array of satisfying and exotic choices.

Sauces will transform a bland, everyday meal into an exotic masterpiece of contrasting flavors, aromas, textures, and colors. Served as a relish, sauce, or condiment, cold or warm salsas will enliven your meals with elegance, flair, and scintillating flavor. Just a spoonful of salsa will readily perk up any ordinary, bland dish. A rich, spicy, red salsa can enhance a dish of eggs, smother tender chunks of beef, or attractively adorn a plate of enchiladas. Try a tangy, piquant green salsa to spice up a platter of vegetables or enrich a serving of seafood, chicken, or beef.

In *Mexican Sauces*, you will discover several easy-to-prepare recipes that offer an enticing collection of delicious and attractive sauces. The fresh vegetables, fruits, herbs, and other seasonings blend to give a distinctive flavor to each sauce. Red and green chiles provide the zest to most of the sauces presented here. In Mexico, dedicated cooks shop for their chiles in markets where the stalls overflow with mounds of colorful red and green chiles. In America, we are beginning to see a greater selection of chiles offered in most large grocery markets. You can also find chiles in mail-order catalogs, if you cannot find them in your local market.

Every cook should have their favorite sauce for their collection of special recipes. With these low-calorie and lowfat sauce recipes, you too can concoct magic potions to impress your family and friends. If you regularly use lots of salsa, you might want to make larger quantities of your favorite sauce. If you do, increase each sauce recipe as you like and refrigerate for up to a week or freeze it in a large, tightly sealed plastic jar or bottle.

Mexican Sauces

14

—❧—

Ranch Sauce
(Salsa Ranchera)

Preparation time: 20 minutes

You won't taste a Mexican chile sauce that isn't memorable. This spicy, red, country-style tomato sauce is refreshing and complements many different Mexican meals. Ranch Sauce is especially wonderful with eggs, enchiladas, and rice. If you like spicy treats, add a whole jalapeño chile for an even spicier, livelier sauce.

1 medium white onion, chopped
$\frac{1}{2}$ cup green onions, finely sliced
1 to 3 cloves garlic, crushed in a garlic press
$\frac{1}{8}$ to 1 fresh serrano or jalapeño chile, seeded, washed, and finely chopped (optional, for a spicier dish)
5 medium ripe tomatoes, blanched or roasted, peeled, seeded, and finely chopped
$\frac{1}{2}$ cup low-salt broth
1 teaspoon fresh oregano, minced
4 to 8 sprigs fresh cilantro, minced
salt and freshly ground pepper

Sauté the white and green onions, garlic, and chile with 2 tablespoons of water in a skillet over medium-high heat until onions become tender and transparent; reduce heat to low. Add tomatoes and cook 2 minutes. Purée the sautéed onion and tomato mixture, broth, oregano, and cilantro in a blender. Salt and pepper the sauce according to individual taste. Serve hot or cold.

Makes 4 to 5 cups

Each ¼-cup serving provides:

14	Calories	3 g	Carbohydrate
1 g	Protein	6 mg	Sodium
0 g	Fat	0 mg	Cholesterol

15

※

Green Chile Sauce
(Salsa Verde)

Preparation time: 20 minutes

This is a spicy, versatile Green Chile Sauce with a special tangy blend of lime juice and tomatoes. To enhance the spiciness of this salsa, add more serrano or jalapeño chiles for a special, spicy treat. This recipe makes lots of sauce. Refrigerate the sauce in tightly sealed glass jars for later use with many of the recipes found in this cookbook.

2 to 6 fresh anaheim chiles
1 medium white onion, diced
1 to 2 cloves garlic, crushed in a garlic press
1/8 to 1 fresh serrano or jalapeño chile, seeded,
    washed, and finely chopped (optional, for
    a spicier dish)
3 small ripe tomatoes, chopped
1 cup low-salt broth
2 to 4 sprigs fresh cilantro
2 tablespoons lime juice
1 tablespoon apple cider vinegar
salt and freshly ground pepper

Preheat the broiler. Roast the anaheim chiles 2 to 3 inches under the broiler 3 to 4 minutes on each side. Occasionally rotate the chiles until evenly browned and blistered on each side. Put the chiles in a tightly closed plastic bag to steam for 5 minutes. Carefully peel off the charred skin. Cut off the stem, seed, rinse, and finely chop the chiles; set aside.

Sauté the white onion, garlic, and serrano chile with 2 tablespoons of water in a skillet over medium-high heat until the onions become tender and transparent; reduce heat to low. Add tomatoes and cook 2 minutes. Purée the sautéed onion and tomato mixture, anaheim chiles, broth, cilantro, lime juice, and apple cider vinegar in a blender. Salt and pepper the sauce according to individual taste. Serve hot or cold.

Makes 4¹/₂ to 5 cups

Each ¹/₄-cup serving provides:

9	Calories	2 g	Carbohydrate
0 g	Protein	3 mg	Sodium
0 g	Fat	0 mg	Cholesterol

16

※

Red Chile Sauce
(*Salsa de Chile Rojo*)

Preparation time: 30 minutes
Chile soaking time: 60 minutes

The dried ancho chile creates a deep-colored, rich-flavored sauce that is popular throughout Mexico. Easily stored in quantity, this is a versatile sauce used often in the recipes found in this cookbook. Simmer poultry, beef, or seafood in this zesty sauce for a memorable, savory meal. For another delightful treat, use this piquant sauce to smother your enchiladas and burritos with full flavor. For a less spicy, thinner sauce, reduce the number of ancho, anaheim, or dried red chiles you use.

2 to 3 ancho or other dried red chiles, coarsely
      shredded and seeded with stems removed
2 to 4 fresh anaheim chiles
2 small ripe tomatoes, blanched or roasted, peeled
      and finely chopped
1/8 to 1 fresh serrano or jalapeño chile, seeded,
      washed, and finely chopped (optional, for
      a spicier dish)
1 medium white onion, diced
1/2 cup green onions, finely sliced
1 to 2 cloves garlic, crushed in a garlic press
2 cups low-salt broth
1/2 cup water
2 to 4 sprigs fresh cilantro, minced (optional)
2 teaspoons fresh oregano, minced
salt and freshly ground pepper

Rinse the ancho chiles. Toast the ancho chiles in a hot skillet for 5 minutes. Cover the chiles with boiling water and soak for at least 1 hour. Drain well; set aside.

Preheat the broiler. Roast the anaheim chiles 2 to 3 inches under the broiler 3 to 4 minutes on each side. Occasionally rotate the chiles until they evenly brown and blister on each side. Put the chiles in a tightly closed plastic bag to steam for 5 minutes. Carefully peel off the charred skin. Cut off the stems, seed, rinse, and finely chop the chiles. Purée the ancho and anaheim chiles and remaining ingredients in a blender until smooth. Salt and pepper the sauce according to individual taste. Simmer the purée in a saucepan over low heat for 10 minutes.

Makes 5 to 6 cups

Each ¼-cup serving provides:

10	Calories	2 g	Carbohydrate
0 g	Protein	4 mg	Sodium
0 g	Fat	0 mg	Cholesterol

17

—✦—

Mexican Tomato Sauce

(Salsa de Jitomate)

Preparation time: 15 minutes

Salsa is an integral part of the Mexican kitchen! It has
played an important cultural role since before the time of
the Aztecs. Sauces, such as this one, embellish most
Mexican dishes. The red and green colors will make
every dish more attractive. If you like, make this sauce in
advance and store it in the refrigerator. I usually make
large quantities of this versatile, flavorful sauce and store
it in tightly sealed jars for later use. Try roasting the chiles
or onions to give your salsa a distinct, nuttier flavor. For a
spicier sauce, increase the number of chiles.

1 fresh anaheim chile
1 medium white onion, finely diced
$1/2$ cup green onions, finely sliced
2 to 3 cloves garlic, crushed in a garlic press
$1/8$ to 1 fresh serrano or jalapeño chile, seeded,
    washed, and finely chopped (optional, for
    a spicier dish)
5 medium ripe tomatoes, blanched or roasted,
    peeled and chopped
1 to 3 sprigs fresh cilantro, minced
salt and freshly ground pepper

Preheat the broiler. Roast the anaheim chile 2 to 3 inches
under the broiler 3 to 4 minutes on each side. Occasionally rotate the chile until it evenly browns and blisters on
each side. Put the chile in a tightly closed plastic bag to

steam for 5 minutes. Carefully peel off the charred skin. Cut off the stem, seed, rinse, and finely chop.

Sauté the white and green onions, garlic, and anaheim and serrano chiles with 2 tablespoons of water in a skillet over medium heat until the onions become tender and transparent; reduce heat to medium-low. Add tomatoes and cook gently for 5 minutes. Purée 1 cup of the cooked sauce mixture and cilantro in a blender. Mix the purée and remaining cooked tomato mixture in a medium-size bowl; mix well. Salt and pepper the dish according to individual taste. Serve the sauce hot or cold.

Makes 4 to 4¹/2 cups

Each ¹/4-cup serving provides:

15	Calories	3 g	Carbohydrate
1 g	Protein	6 mg	Sodium
0 g	Fat	0 mg	Cholesterol

18

—❧—

Tomatillo Sauce
(Salsa de Tomatillo)

Preparation time: 15 minutes

Popular in Mexico, this tangy, green sauce is served most
often with poultry or fish. It's also delicious served as a
dip or with tacos, burritos, and enchiladas. This particular version is rather mild yet still manages to leave a
delightfully tangy aftertaste. Add the seeds from an anaheim chile if you would like to make the sauce even more
sensational.

2 to 3 fresh, anaheim chiles
1 small white onion, diced
1 to 2 cloves garlic, crushed in a garlic press
1/8 to 1 fresh serrano or jalapeño chile, chopped with
    seeds (optional, for a spicier dish)
5 medium tomatillos, husked and chopped
    (about 3 cups)
1 cup low-salt broth
1 tablespoon lime juice
1 tablespoon apple cider vinegar
1 teaspoon fresh oregano, minced
1/4 cup sprigs fresh cilantro, minced
salt and freshly ground pepper

Preheat the broiler. Roast the anaheim chiles 2 to 3 inches
under the broiler 3 to 4 minutes on each side. Occasionally rotate each chile until it evenly browns and blisters
on each side. Put the chiles in a tightly closed plastic bag

to steam for 5 minutes. Carefully peel off the charred skin. Cut off the stem, seed, rinse, and finely chop.

Sauté the onion, garlic, and anaheim and serrano chiles with 2 tablespoons of water over medium heat in a 3-quart saucepan until the onions become tender. Add the tomatillos, broth, lime juice, apple cider vinegar, and oregano; reduce heat to low. Simmer sauce for 5 minutes, stirring occasionally. Add cilantro. Blend the Tomatillo Sauce in a blender until smooth. Salt and pepper according to individual taste. Serve hot or cold.

Makes 2¹/₂ to 3 cups

Each ¹/₄-cup serving provides:			
13	Calories	3 g	Carbohydrate
1 g	Protein	3 mg	Sodium
0 g	Fat	0 mg	Cholesterol

19

—❧—

Fresh Chile Sauce
(Salsa Fresca)

Preparation time: 15 minutes

This refreshing salsa is as common as salt and pepper in most Mexican kitchens and increasingly popular throughout the United States. The fresh, red tomatoes and green chiles blend to create a crimson-colored vision of fresh and exquisite flavor. Now you can make fresh salsa in your own home. Like all Mexican salsa, this versatile recipe can be made in advance and refrigerated in tightly sealed glass jars for later use. For variation, add fresh corn or other seasonal vegetables. This salsa is also great as a dipping sauce for chips and vegetables.

2 fresh anaheim chiles
5 medium ripe tomatoes, finely chopped
1 to 2 cloves garlic, crushed in a garlic press
2 to 5 sprigs fresh cilantro, minced
$\frac{1}{8}$ to 1 fresh serrano or jalapeño chile, seeded,
    washed, and finely chopped (optional, for
    a spicier dish)
1 small white onion, diced
$\frac{1}{2}$ cup green onions, finely sliced
5 teaspoons lime juice
4 teaspoons apple cider vinegar
salt and freshly ground pepper

Preheat the broiler. Roast the anaheim chiles 2 to 3 inches under the broiler 3 to 4 minutes on each side. Occasionally rotate the chiles until they evenly brown and blister on each side. Put chiles in a tightly closed plastic bag to steam for 5 minutes. Carefully peel off charred skin. Cut off the stem, seed, rinse, and finely chop; set aside.

Coarsely blend together 1½ cups of the chopped tomatoes, garlic, cilantro, and serrano chile in a blender. Put the tomato purée in a medium-size bowl with the white and green onions, lime juice, and apple cider vinegar. Add remaining tomatoes to the bowl; mix well. Salt and pepper the salsa according to individual taste. Serve cold.

Makes 4 cups

Each ¼-cup serving provides:

16	Calories	5 g	Carbohydrate
1 g	Protein	9 mg	Sodium
0 g	Fat	0 mg	Cholesterol

20

—✤—

Pasilla Chile Sauce
(Salsa de Chile Pasilla)

Preparation time: 15 minutes
Chile soaking time: 60 minutes

The pasilla chile is a large, black, piquant chile that creates a thick, savory, reddish-orange sauce great for many Mexican dishes. This sauce offers a sensational, tangy flavor and easily stores in large quantity for later use. Pasilla sauces are superb blended with seafood, enchiladas, and burritos.

1 dried pasilla chile, coarsely shredded and seeded
    with stem removed
1 dried ancho chile, coarsely shredded and seeded
    with stem removed
2 fresh anaheim chiles
1 medium white onion, diced
1 to 2 cloves garlic, crushed in a garlic press
$1/8$ to 1 fresh serrano or jalapeño chile, seeded,
    washed, and finely chopped (optional, for
    a spicier dish)
2 medium ripe tomatoes, blanched or roasted, peeled
    and chopped
1 tablespoon apple cider vinegar
2 tablespoons lime juice
2 to 4 sprigs fresh cilantro, minced (optional)
2 teaspoons fresh oregano, minced
2 cups low-salt broth
salt and freshly ground pepper

Toast the pasilla and ancho chiles on all sides in a hot skillet for 5 minutes. Remove from heat. Cover the chiles with boiling water and soak for at least 1 hour. Drain and rinse the chiles well; set aside.

Preheat broiler. Roast the anaheim chiles 2 to 3 inches under the broiler 3 to 4 minutes on each side. Occasionally rotate the chiles until they evenly brown and blister on each side. Put the chiles in a tightly closed plastic bag to steam for 5 minutes. Carefully peel off the charred skin. Cut off the stem, seed, rinse, and finely chop.

Blend the pasilla, ancho, and anaheim chiles and remaining ingredients in a blender until the purée is smooth. Salt and pepper the sauce according to individual taste.

Makes 5 cups

Each ¼-cup serving provides:

12	Calories	3 g	Carbohydrate
0 g	Protein	4 mg	Sodium
1 g	Fat	0 mg	Cholesterol

21

—❧—

Chile Salad Dressing

(Adevezo para Ensalada)

Preparation time: 10 minutes
Refrigeration time: 15 minutes

Put away the store-bought salad dressings forever! This
salad dressing is low-calorie, lowfat and especially
piquant! Now you can eat the dressing that you want
without worrying about the calories. For a tempting variation and a creamier dressing, try adding some fat-free
cottage cheese or yogurt.

2 tablespoons lime juice
1 tablespoon apple cider vinegar
1 tablespoon water
3 tablespoons Green Chile Sauce (Recipe #15)
1 clove garlic, crushed in a garlic press
$\frac{1}{8}$ to 1 fresh serrano or jalapeño chile, seeded,
    washed, and finely chopped (optional, for
    a spicier dish)
1 teaspoon fresh oregano, minced
1 to 4 sprigs fresh cilantro, minced
salt and freshly ground pepper

Combine all the ingredients in a jar with a tight-fitting lid.
Salt and pepper the dressing according to individual taste.
Cover; shake the dressing to blend thoroughly. Refrigerate

for 15 minutes. Shake the salad dressing again before serving.

Makes ¹/₃ cup

Each 1 tablespoon-serving provides:

7	Calories	2 g	Carbohydrate
0 g	Protein	6 mg	Sodium
0 g	Fat	0 mg	Cholesterol

22

—⚜—

Fresh Papaya Sauce
(Salsa Fresca de Papaya)

Preparation time: 15 minutes
Refrigeration time: 15 minutes

Serve this delightfully refreshing salsa of tropical fruits
alone, as a special dessert, over cereal, cottage cheese, or
yogurt or as a refreshing salad dressing over lettuce. Easy
to prepare in advance, this simple fruit salsa offers a wonderfully smooth and luscious low-calorie treat. For an
equally delicious variation, decrease the papaya to 1 cup
and increase pineapple to 2 cups.

2 cups ripe papaya, cut into 1-inch pieces
1 cup ripe pineapple, cut into 1-inch pieces
$^1/_2$ cup ripe bananas, sliced into 1-inch pieces
$^1/_2$ cup cherries, pitted
1 small kiwi, peeled, cut in half, and finely sliced

Combine all the ingredients, excluding the cherries and kiwi
in a small bowl; mix gently to coat the fruit with the juices.
Purée one-third of the fruit mixture in a blender. Return the
purée to the bowl of remaining fruit. Stir in cherries and
kiwi; mix well. Refrigerate 15 minutes. Serve cold.

Makes 3 cups

Each $^1/_4$-cup serving provides:

63	Calories	23 g	Carbohydrate
1 g	Protein	3 mg	Sodium
1 g	Fat	0 mg	Cholesterol

Mexican Egg Dishes

Eggs, called *huevos* in Spanish, are a favorite for an appetizing, fulfilling Mexican meal. Mexican egg dishes are delicious, filling, and nutritious. If you want to energize your taste buds in the morning, try a Mexican breakfast composed of light, fluffy eggs and a piquant, full-flavored sauce. Popular throughout Mexico, you will find regional egg dishes offered by restaurants throughout the country. In the sixteenth century, the Spaniards originally introduced the chicken egg to the local Indians who subsequently embraced traditional Spanish egg dishes with enthusiasm. As a result, the Indians quickly assimilated the new egg dishes into their spicy diet.

Eggs provide plenty of protein, vitamins, and minerals for your healthful diet. Red and green chiles, rich in vitamin C, will add zest and zing to most of these nutritious dishes. If you want to limit the number of eggs you eat because of their high cholesterol content, try using a whole-egg substitute. Most of these recipes recommend the use of whole-egg substitutes to significantly reduce the amount of cholesterol and fat. Most grocery markets stock egg substitutes in the refrigerated section next to the eggs.

Many classic Mexican egg dishes surely deserve an award for the most satisfying, legendary breakfasts served anywhere in the world. The recipes in *Mexican Egg Dishes* offer an enticing assortment of delicious and attractive meals. You can serve these uncomplicated, versatile dishes any time of day with little fuss. Elegantly or informally served, these eye-appealing dishes will contribute to a lazy brunch, light luncheon, one-dish dinner, or irresistible late-night snack. Egg dishes reach even greater culinary heights when laced with the delicate, blended flavors of chiles, herbs, and tomatoes. Served with fresh fruits and a glass of juice, you can enjoy this simple but savory fare. You won't have to look farther than the next few pages for an array of ideal, great-tasting egg dishes for you, your family, and friends.

Mexican Egg Dishes

23

—❦—

Scrambled Eggs with Mushrooms

(Huevos Revueltos con Hongos)

Preparation time: 25 minutes

Scrambled egg dishes are flavorful, easy to prepare, and universally appealing. This particularly pleasing scrambled egg dish features the blended flavors of light and fluffy scrambled eggs smothered with sautéed mushrooms and chiles. Try this dish for a satisfying breakfast, lunch, dinner—or even a late-night snack. It is quick to prepare and very elegant. You can vary this recipe by substituting the mushrooms with other vegetables in season. *Note!* To substantially reduce cholesterol and fat, replace 1 to 3 eggs with a whole-egg substitute (without fat and cholesterol). You won't even notice a difference in taste or texture!

8 medium eggs
nonstick pan coating
2 sprigs fresh cilantro, minced (optional)
1 cup green onions, finely sliced
$1/8$ to 1 fresh serrano or jalapeño chile, seeded,
    washed, and finely chopped (optional, for
    a spicier dish)
3 cups mushrooms, chopped
3 tablespoons Green Chile Sauce (Recipe #15)
salt and freshly ground pepper

Remove the eggs from the refrigerator to adjust to room temperature. Evenly spray a large skillet with nonstick pan coating, entirely covering the bottom of the skillet so eggs will not stick; set skillet aside.

Sauté the cilantro, green onion, serrano chile, mushrooms, and Green Chile Sauce with 2 tablespoons of water over medium-high heat in a small saucepan. Stir mixture frequently until mushrooms are just tender. Remove saucepan from burner; set aside.

Heat the prepared skillet over medium heat until just hot. Whip the eggs in a small bowl until well blended. Pour whipped eggs into hot skillet; reduce heat to low. Gently stir the eggs to scramble them until creamy and set. Spread one-sixth portion of the scrambled eggs on six oven-warmed plates. Attractively cover each portion of the scrambled eggs with one-sixth of the mushroom mixture. Serve the hot scrambled eggs immediately.

Serves 6

Each serving provides:

110	Calories	5 g	Carbohydrate
9 g	Protein	82 mg	Sodium
6 g	Fat	253 mg	Cholesterol

24

—✳—

Eggs Poached in Ranch Sauce
(Huevos en Salsa Ranchera)

Preparation time: 10 minutes
Cooking time: 7 to 8 minutes

This is a low-calorie version of an eye-appealing Mexican
dish highlighting fresh eggs slowly poached in a thick,
spicy red sauce. The sauce infuses the eggs with the
piquant flavors of chiles, onions, and tomatoes. The rich
combination of Ranch Sauce and poached eggs is a delightfully tantalizing and easy-to-prepare meal. Try this light
and versatile dish for breakfast, brunch, lunch, dinner, or
late-night snack. For another version, try poaching the
eggs in a savory Red (#16) or Green (#15) Chile Sauce.

6 medium eggs
2 cups Ranch Sauce (Recipe #14)
¼ cup green onions, finely sliced
6 sprigs fresh cilantro
salt and freshly ground pepper

Remove eggs from refrigerator to adjust to room temperature. Warm the Ranch Sauce in a large skillet over
medium heat until just before sauce reaches the boiling
point; reduce heat to low. Break the eggs one by one on a
plate and carefully slide the eggs into the hot sauce.
Cover; cook the eggs for 3 minutes. Turn off the heat and
continue to cook the eggs (still covered) until the whites
set according to individual taste.

To serve, slide an egg onto each oven-warmed plate.
Spoon remaining sauce in a circle around the two eggs on

each plate. Sprinkle each egg serving with green onions. Salt and pepper the dish according to individual taste. Serve the hot egg dish immediately. Garnish each plate with fresh cilantro sprigs.

Serves 6

Each serving provides:

91	Calories	6 g	Carbohydrate
7 g	Protein	68 mg	Sodium
4 g	Fat	190 mg	Cholesterol

25

❧

Mexican-style Baked Eggs
(Huevos a la Mexicana)

Preparation time: 15 minutes
Baking time: 15 to 20 minutes
Preheat oven to 350°

This is an eye-appealing Mexican egg dish and a flavorful variation of the recipe for Rancher's Eggs (*Huevos Rancheros*, #26). In this recipe the eggs are baked in their individual pools of thick, red, spicy sauce nested on a corn tortilla. The spicy, rich-tasting combination of Ranch Sauce and baked eggs is easy to prepare and a festive surprise for a lazy, late-morning Sunday brunch. For another variation, use Green Chile Sauce (#15).

6 medium eggs
nonstick pan coating
1 fresh anaheim chile
$^1/_2$ cup white onions, finely chopped
$^1/_2$ cup green onions, finely sliced
$^1/_8$ to 1 fresh serrano or jalapeño chile, seeded, washed,
    and finely chopped (optional, for a spicier dish)
1 small ripe tomato, blanched or roasted, peeled, and
    finely chopped
1 cup Ranch Sauce (Recipe #14)
2 sprigs fresh cilantro, minced (optional)
6 corn tortillas
salt and freshly ground pepper

Remove the eggs from the refrigerator so that they can warm to room temperature. Spray a large baking sheet with a nonstick pan coating, entirely covering the bottom of the baking sheet so tortillas will not stick; set baking sheet aside.

Preheat the broiler. Roast the anaheim chile 2 to 3 inches under the broiler for 3 to 4 minutes on each side. Occasionally rotate chile until it evenly browns and blisters on all sides. Put the chile in a tightly closed plastic bag to steam for 5 minutes. Carefully peel off the charred skin. Cut off the stem, seed, rinse, and chop.

Sauté the white and green onions and serrano and anaheim chiles with 2 tablespoons of water in a large skillet over medium-high heat until the onions become tender. Add the tomato; reduce heat to low. Add Ranch Sauce and cilantro; continue to cook for 2 minutes. Lay the six corn tortillas flat on the prepared baking sheet. Cover each tortilla entirely with one-sixth portion of the cooked Ranch Sauce mixture. Use a teaspoon to push the sauce to the outside edge of each corn tortilla to make a ring. Build the sides of the "red nest" high enough to contain a raw egg in the center of the sauce. Carefully break an egg in the center of each tortilla. Ensure that the "nest" holds the contents of each egg within its wall of sauce. Do not allow the egg yolk to break or let the egg white drip past the "nest" onto the baking sheet.

Bake the eggs in preheated oven for 17 to 20 minutes, until the eggs set according to individual taste. Remove the baking sheet from the oven. Use a spatula to place the individual corn tortillas on six oven-warmed plates. Salt and pepper the dish according to individual taste. Garnish each portion with freshly ground pepper.

Serves 6

<table>
<tr><td colspan="4">Each serving provides:</td></tr>
<tr><td>140</td><td>Calories</td><td>15 g</td><td>Carbohydrate</td></tr>
<tr><td>8 g</td><td>Protein</td><td>89 mg</td><td>Sodium</td></tr>
<tr><td>4 g</td><td>Fat</td><td>190 mg</td><td>Cholesterol</td></tr>
</table>

26

—❦—

Rancher's Eggs
(Huevos Rancheros)

Preparation time: 15 minutes
Preheat oven to 350°

This classic, piquant egg dish is popular throughout
Mexico and often served in many American restaurants.
The spicy, aromatic flavors of the Ranch Sauce and fried
eggs are the perfect match to create an exceptional meal.
Serve this appealing, versatile dish as an eye-opening,
late-morning meal, light main course for lunch, or even a
savory late-night snack.

6 medium eggs
1¹/₂ cups Ranch Sauce (Recipe #14)
3 corn tortillas
nonstick pan coating
¹/₃ cup green onions, finely sliced
6 sprigs fresh cilantro
salt and freshly ground pepper

Remove the eggs from the refrigerator to adjust to room
temperature. Warm the Ranch Sauce over low heat in a
small saucepan; stir occasionally. Tightly wrap the tortillas in foil. Warm the tortillas in a preheated oven for 5
minutes until the tortillas are soft and pliable; set tortillas
aside wrapped in foil.
    Evenly spray a large skillet with nonstick pan coat-
ing, entirely covering the bottom of the skillet so eggs will
not stick. Heat skillet over medium-high heat until just
hot; reduce heat to medium. Gently drop each egg into

the skillet. Cook eggs until the whites set. Gently flip each egg with a spatula. Do not break the yolk. Cook until the yolks set according to individual taste.

Cut the tortillas in half. Place half of a warmed tortilla on an oven-warmed plate. Attractively spread ¼ cup of the warmed Ranch Sauce over the half of tortilla. Arrange the Ranch sauce in a circle half on and half off the tortilla. Use a spatula to carefully slide a fried egg atop each pool of Ranchera Sauce on the tortillas. Salt and pepper the eggs according to individual taste. Garnish each dish with fresh green onions and fresh sprigs of cilantro. Serve the hot eggs immediately.

Serves 6

Each serving provides:

109	Calories	9 g	Carbohydrate
7 g	Protein	26 mg	Sodium
4 g	Fat	190 mg	Cholesterol

27

❧

Breakfast Egg Burritos
(Burritos de Huevos)

Preparation time: 15 minutes
Preheat oven to 350°

Delicious and easy to prepare, this egg dish is perfect for a quick, nutritious breakfast, late brunch, or late-night snack. Snugly wrapped in a soft, warm flour tortilla, this spicy egg burrito is a flavorful and substantial breakfast. Children will love holding this warm sandwich stuffed with light, fluffy eggs. Dedicated egg lovers will applaud the enticing combination of chiles, mushrooms, and eggs that tastes great even when eaten on the run. You can make these burritos in advance, store them in a plastic bag, then warm them later in the microwave. *Note!* To substantially reduce cholesterol and fat, replace 1 to 3 eggs with a whole-egg substitute (without fat and cholesterol). You won't even notice a difference in taste or texture!

5 medium eggs
6 fresh lowfat flour tortillas (6-inch)
nonstick pan coating
¼ cup white onions, chopped
¼ cup green onions, chopped
½ cup mushrooms, chopped
2 sprigs fresh cilantro, minced (optional)
¼ cup Green Chile Sauce (Recipe #15)
salt and freshly ground pepper

Remove the eggs from the refrigerator to adjust to room temperature. Wrap the flour tortillas in foil and warm in a preheated oven for 5 minutes until the tortillas are soft and pliable. Evenly spray a large skillet with nonstick pan coating, entirely covering the bottom of the skillet so eggs will not stick; set skillet aside.

Sauté the white and green onions and mushrooms in a small saucepan with 2 tablespoons of water until the onions become tender and transparent; reduce heat to low. Stir in the cilantro and Green Chile Sauce. Heat the prepared skillet over medium-high heat until just hot. Whip the eggs in a small bowl until light and well blended. Pour the whipped eggs into the skillet; reduce heat to low. Gently stir the eggs to scramble them until they set according to individual taste. Place one-sixth portion of the scrambled egg mixture in the center of each warm tortilla. Top the eggs with one-sixth portion of the onion and mushroom mixture. Fold the sides inward to form a rectangular burrito. Salt and pepper the dish according to individual taste. Serve the hot egg burritos immediately.

Serves 6

Each serving provides:

140	Calories	19 g	Carbohydrate
7 g	Protein	78 mg	Sodium
4 g	Fat	158 mg	Cholesterol

28

——— ❧ ———

Spanish Omelet
(Tortilla Española)

Preparation time: 20 minutes

In Spain, an omelet is actually called a *tortilla*. While traveling through Spain, my family stopped to eat dinner at a local restaurant. My father, who enjoys a tortilla with his meal, ordered one to accompany his first Spanish meal (meaning the Mexican flatbread kind of tortilla made with corn or flour). You can imagine our surprise when the waiter served my father's dinner with a tortilla—a huge Spanish omelet smothered in potatoes. The waiter probably thought we were all crazy as we burst out laughing at the incredulous look on my father's face! *Note!* To substantially reduce cholesterol and fat, replace 1 to 3 eggs with a whole-egg substitute (without fat and cholesterol). You won't even notice a difference in taste or texture!

5 medium eggs
nonstick pan coating
¼ cup white onions, thinly sliced
½ cup green onions, finely sliced
¾ cup potatoes, pared, cooked, and coarsely chopped
1 small, fresh anaheim chile, seeded, washed, and
     finely chopped
¼ cup red bell peppers, halved, seeded, washed, and
     finely chopped
⅓ cup Green Chile Sauce (Recipe #15)
2 to 4 sprigs fresh cilantro, minced
4 tomato wedges
salt and freshly ground pepper

Remove the eggs from the refrigerator to adjust to room temperature. Evenly spray a large skillet with non-stick pan coating, entirely covering the bottom of the skillet so eggs will not stick.

Sauté the white and green onions, potatoes, anaheim chile, and red bell peppers with 2 tablespoons of water in the prepared skillet over medium-high heat until the white onions become tender; stir frequently. Stir in the Green Chile Sauce; reduce heat to medium low.

Whip the eggs in a small bowl until well blended. Evenly pour the whipped eggs into the skillet over the potatoes. Roll the eggs to cover the entire surface of the skillet; reduce heat to low. Gently prick the omelet with the edge of a spatula to let the uncooked egg run to the bottom of the skillet. Continue to cook the eggs for 3 minutes. Cover the skillet; cook for 1 to 2 minutes more, until the eggs are creamy and set on the surface. Salt and pepper the omelet according to individual taste.

When you remove the omelet from the skillet, do not fold. Cut the omelet into six wedges. Use a spatula to loosen the omelet from the pan. Remove the individual omelet wedges from the skillet onto an oven-warmed platter. The omelet should retain the shape of a flat tortilla. Serve the omelets immediately. Garnish each dish with fresh minced cilantro and tomato wedges.

Serves 6

Each wedge provides:

86	Calories	15 g	Carbohydrate
12 g	Protein	110 mg	Sodium
7 g	Fat	317 mg	Cholesterol

29

❦

Mexican Omelet

(Tortilla a la Mexicana)

Preparation time: 20 minutes

Visit any restaurant throughout Mexico and you will probably find at least one special omelet included on the menu. Typically, you will find these light, fluffy omelets blended with piquant chiles and sauces. In any home or restaurant, there is always a special occasion to enjoy an appetizing omelet. Create a festive atmosphere for breakfast with this delicious omelet made with a colorful, full-flavored red sauce. To complete this delicious breakfast, serve the omelet with a tortilla or thin slice of toast. Don't forget to set a small bowl of extra salsa on the side for salsa lovers. *Note!* To substantially reduce cholesterol and fat, replace 1 to 3 eggs with a whole-egg substitute (without fat and cholesterol). You won't even notice a difference in taste or texture!

5 medium eggs
nonstick pan coating
5 tablespoons Mexican Tomato Sauce (Recipe # 17)
1 fresh anaheim chile, seeded, washed, and
    thinly sliced
³/₄ cup green onions, finely sliced
2 sprigs fresh cilantro, minced (optional)
salt and freshly ground pepper

Remove the eggs from the refrigerator to adjust to room temperature. Evenly spray a large skillet with nonstick pan coating, entirely covering the bottom of the skillet so eggs will not stick; set skillet aside.

Heat the Mexican Tomato Sauce and anaheim chiles in a small saucepan over medium heat for 2 minutes; reduce heat to low.

Heat the prepared skillet over medium-high heat until just hot. Whip the eggs in a small bowl until well blended. Pour one-fourth portion of the whipped eggs into skillet; reduce heat to low. Spread the eggs with a spatula to cover the entire surface of the skillet. Gently scrape the bottom of the skillet a few times to let the uncooked egg run to the bottom. Continue to cook the eggs until they are creamy and set. Salt and pepper the omelet according to individual taste.

Evenly spread one-fourth portion of the Mexican Tomato Sauce and 2 tablespoons of the green onions and chiles across the flat omelet. Fold the omelet in half by lifting one side of the omelet over to cover the filling. Using a spatula to loosen the omelet from the pan, slide the cooked omelet from the skillet onto an oven-warmed plate. Repeat this process to cook three more omelets. Garnish the omelets with the remaining green onions and fresh minced cilantro. Serve the hot omelets immediately.

Serves 4

Each serving provides:

103	Calories	5 g	Carbohydrate
8 g	Protein	81 mg	Sodium
5 g	Fat	238 mg	Cholesterol

30

—❦—

Scrambled Ranch Eggs
(Huevos Revueltos en Salsa Ranchera)

Preparation time: 20 minutes

Ketchup lovers, you will throw away your bottle of
ketchup when you eat these scrambled eggs! Try this
enticing combination of tomatoes and chiles with eggs. In
this recipe, the light, moist eggs blend well with the fresh,
tangy flavors of the Ranch Sauce. Green onions and
freshly ground pepper provide a pleasing garnish to dis-
tinguish this attractive scrambled egg dish. *Note!* To substantially reduce cholesterol and fat, replace 1 to 3 eggs
with a whole-egg substitute (without fat and cholesterol).
You won't even notice a difference in taste or texture!

6 medium eggs
nonstick pan coating
$^1/_4$ cup white onion, diced
$^3/_4$ cup green onions, finely sliced
$^1/_8$ to 1 fresh serrano or jalapeño chile, seeded,
    washed, and finely chopped (optional, for
    a spicier dish)
$1^1/_2$ cups Ranch Sauce (Recipe #14)
6 sprigs fresh cilantro
salt and freshly ground pepper

Remove the eggs from the refrigerator to adjust to room
temperature. Evenly spray a large skillet with nonstick
pan coating, entirely covering the bottom of the skillet so
eggs will not stick; set skillet aside.

In a saucepan, sauté the white onion, ¹/₂ cup of the green onions, and serrano chile with 2 tablespoons of water over medium-high heat until the onions become tender. Add Ranch Sauce; reduce heat to low. Heat the prepared skillet over medium-high heat until just hot. Whip the eggs in a small bowl until well blended. Pour the whipped eggs into the hot skillet; reduce the heat to low. Gently stir the eggs to scramble them until the eggs are creamy and set.

Thinly spread one-sixth portion of the Ranch Sauce mixture on six oven-warmed plates. Attractively arrange the scrambled eggs in equal portions over the Ranch Sauce on the plates. Sprinkle the remaining green onions on top of the eggs. Salt and pepper the eggs according to individual taste. Garnish the center of each plate with the fresh cilantro sprigs.

Serves 6

Each serving provides:

80	Calories	6 g	Carbohydrate
6 g	Protein	58 mg	Sodium
4 g	Fat	158 mg	Cholesterol

31

Scrambled Eggs with Green Chile Sauce

(Huevos Revueltos en Salsa Verde)

Preparation time: 15 minutes

This decorative scrambled egg dish, blended with a piquant green sauce, tastes just as good as it looks. Simple and quick to prepare, these delicious, fluffy eggs are nevertheless a satisfying dish at any time of the day or night. Use Red Chile Sauce (#16) as an alternative to the Green Chile Sauce if you want to try a pleasing variation of this elegant scrambled egg dish. *Note!* To substantially reduce cholesterol and fat, replace 1 to 3 eggs with a whole-egg substitute (without fat and cholesterol). You won't even notice a difference in taste or texture!

6 medium eggs
nonstick pan coating
3 tablespoons Green Chile Sauce (Recipe #15)
¼ cup green onions, finely sliced
2 to 4 sprigs fresh cilantro, minced (optional)
salt and freshly ground pepper

Remove the eggs from the refrigerator to adjust to room temperature. Evenly spray a large skillet with nonstick pan coating, entirely covering the bottom of the skillet so eggs will not stick.

Heat the prepared skillet over medium heat until just hot. Whip the eggs in a small bowl until well blended. Stir the Green Chile Sauce into the egg mixture; mix well.

Pour the whipped egg mixture into the hot skillet; reduce heat to low. Gently stir the eggs to scramble them until the eggs are creamy and set. Salt and pepper the dish according to individual taste. Serve the hot scrambled eggs immediately on oven-warmed plates. Garnish each plate with the green onions, fresh cilantro, and freshly ground pepper.

Serves 3

Each serving provides:

145	Calories	3 g	Carbohydrate
12 g	Protein	121 mg	Sodium
8 g	Fat	380 mg	Cholesterol

Mexican Tortilla Dishes

When they first came to Mexico in the sixteenth century,
the Spaniards discovered that the native Indians had a
very simple, nutritious diet of corn, beans, squash, chiles,
and wild game. The mainstay of this unique diet was the
mighty corn tortilla. The Spaniards were delighted with
the thin, round, flat cake made from the corn called *matz*.
Indian cooks soaked the corn kernels overnight in lime
then ground the kernels into flour. Pressed into small, flat
cakes, they cooked the tortillas on a hot stone hearth.

Over the years, little has changed. Indians and
Mexicans alike have a deep devotion to their tortillas.
Many Mexican families still make their tortillas by hand.
In the larger towns and cities, most busy Mexican cooks
buy their tortillas from a tortilla factory, called a *tortillería*.
It is the daily job of the youngest Mexican child in the
family to go to the neighborhood *tortillería* to pick up the
tortillas needed for the day's cooking. It's fascinating to
watch the tortilla makers work. They pat the dough into
small balls and place them into a machine where they are
pressed flat, cooked by hot air, and pushed out onto a con-
veyor belt.

Americans have embraced Mexico's time-honored tradition for tortillas with characteristic enthusiasm. Rolled, baked, fried, folded, toasted, steamed, or stacked, these delectable, versatile corn and flour cakes are Mexico's special gift to culinary excellence.

The recipes found in *Mexican Tortilla Dishes* present a classic array of delectable dishes made with tortillas. Elegantly or informally served, these aromatic, spicy tortilla dishes showcase the best of lowfat Mexican cuisine. This section includes recipes to create enchiladas, burritos, tostadas, tacos, and similarly appetizing Mexican delicacies. Fresh, earthy-tasting tortillas, blended with the piquant flavors of chiles, tomatoes, and other ingredients, offer an exciting opportunity for avid cooks to excel and impress.

Mexican Tortilla Dishes

32

※

Bean Burritos

(Burritos de Frijoles)

Preparation time: 20 minutes
Preheat oven to 350°

Combined with the right food, such as corn or rice, beans
are a healthful substitute for beef or other animal protein.
This simple recipe for Mexican burritos combines the
modest bean with chiles and a fresh, warm flour tortilla.
Burritos are the equivalent of the American sandwich
eaten with the hand. This recipe presents the time-honored burrito in its simplest, most nutritious form. Serve
this popular stuffed tortilla with a bowl of Fresh Chile
Sauce (#19) as an easy-to-prepare lunch or as dinner with
rice, a garden-fresh salad, and a bowl of salsa. (For other
salsa recipes, see *Mexican Sauces*.)

6 fresh lowfat flour tortillas (6-inch)
8 sprigs fresh cilantro, (optional)
1 small white onion, finely sliced
$\frac{1}{2}$ cup green onions, finely sliced
1 to 2 cloves garlic, crushed in a garlic press
$\frac{1}{8}$ to 1 fresh serrano or jalapeño chile, seeded,
    washed, and finely chopped (optional, for
    a spicier dish)
1 fresh anaheim chile, seeded, washed, and
    finely chopped
1$\frac{1}{4}$ cups pinto beans, cooked and mashed
1 small ripe tomato, finely chopped
salt and freshly ground pepper

Wrap the flour tortillas in foil. Warm in preheated oven for 5 minutes until the tortillas are soft and pliable. Remove from oven and keep them warm wrapped in the foil; set aside.

Mince 2 sprigs of the cilantro. Cook the white and green onions, garlic, and serrano and anaheim chiles over medium-high heat with 2 tablespoon of water in a large skillet until the onions become tender. Add the pinto beans, tomato, and the 2 sprigs minced cilantro. Simmer the bean mixture uncovered for 1 minute. Salt and pepper to taste.

Evenly spread one-sixth portion of the bean mixture in the middle of each flour tortilla. Roll each tortilla around the filling in a cylinder shape. Place the rolled burritos, seam side down, on oven-warmed plates. Garnish each plate with the remaining fresh cilantro sprigs. Serve hot immediately.

Serves 6

Each serving provides:

133	Calories	28 g	Carbohydrate
6 g	Protein	301 mg	Sodium
1 g	Fat	0 mg	Cholesterol

33

——— ✤ ———

Cheese and Chile Quesadillas

(Quesadillas de Verduras)

Preparation time: 20 minutes
Preheat oven to 350°

This is a popular, easy-to-prepare, stuffed tortilla, called
quesadilla in Spanish. For a less crispy quesadilla, use the
microwave to melt the cheese. Everyone likes to create
their own variation of this simple dish. If you like, try
corn tortillas instead of flour and add steamed zucchini,
corn, or broccoli as equally delicious variations to this
recipe. Serve this tasty stuffed tortilla for lunch or as an
appetizer with a bowl of tasty salsa for dipping. (For salsa
recipes, see *Mexican Sauces*.)

6 fresh lowfat flour tortillas (6-inch)
$^1/_2$ cup white onions, finely chopped
$^1/_4$ cup green onions, finely sliced
1 to 2 cloves garlic, crushed in a garlic press
$^1/_8$ to 1 fresh serrano or jalapeño chile, seeded,
      washed, and finely chopped (optional, for a
      spicier dish)
1 fresh anaheim chile, seeded, washed and
      finely chopped
1 cup mushrooms, sliced
$^1/_2$ cup Mexican Tomato Sauce (Recipe #17)
6 tablespoons lowfat Jack cheese, grated
salt and freshly ground pepper

Wrap the flour tortillas in foil. Warm the tortillas in a preheated oven for 5 minutes until the tortillas are soft and

pliable. Remove from oven and keep warm wrapped in the foil; set aside.

Sauté the white and green onions, garlic, and serrano and anaheim chiles with 1 tablespoon of water in a saucepan over medium-high heat until the onions become tender; stir frequently. Stir in the mushrooms and Mexican Tomato Sauce; cook 2 minutes. Salt and pepper the sauce mixture according to individual taste.

Evenly spread one-sixth portion of the sautéed onion and Mexican Tomato Sauce mixture on the right side of a warm, pliable flour tortilla. Sprinkle 1 tablespoon of the grated cheese over the onion and sauce mixture. Fold the tortilla in half. Repeat the same process with the remaining five flour tortillas; set aside.

Heat a large griddle over high heat until the griddle is very hot; reduce heat to medium. Place the folded tortillas on the hot griddle and brown them on both sides for 2 to 3 minutes until the cheese melts. Cut each tortilla into wedges and serve immediately.

Serves 6

Each serving provides:

130	Calories	20 g	Carbohydrate
7 g	Protein	381 mg	Sodium
4 g	Fat	10 mg	Cholesterol

34

❧

Cheese and Chicken Quesadillas
(Quesadillas de Pollo)

Preparation time: 20 minutes
Preheat oven to 350°

Here is another variation to the easy-to-prepare, popular
quesadilla. For a less crispy quesadilla, use the microwave
to melt the cheese. Serve this tasty, high-protein, stuffed
tortilla for lunch or as an appetizer with a bowl of tasty
salsa for dipping. (For salsa recipes, see *Mexican Sauces.*)
For a satisfying variation, substitute Red Chile Sauce
(#16) for the Green Chile Sauce.

6 fresh lowfat flour tortillas (6 inch)
½ cup white onions, finely chopped
¼ cup green onions, finely sliced
1 to 2 cloves garlic, crushed in a garlic press
1 fresh anaheim chile, seeded, washed, and
    finely chopped
⅛ to 1 fresh serrano or jalapeño chile, seeded,
    washed, and finely chopped (optional, for a
    spicier dish)
⅓ cup extra-lean chicken, cooked and shredded
½ cup Green Chile Sauce (Recipe #15)
6 tablespoons lowfat Jack cheese, grated
salt and freshly ground pepper

Wrap the flour tortillas in foil. Warm the tortillas in preheated oven for 5 minutes until the tortillas are soft and
pliable. Sauté the white and green onions, garlic, and anaheim and serrano chiles with 1 tablespoon of water in a

saucepan over medium-high heat until the onions become tender; stir frequently. Stir in the chicken and Green Chile Sauce; cook for 2 minutes. Salt and pepper the mixture according to individual taste. Remove the saucepan from heat.

Evenly spread one-sixth portion of the sautéed chicken and Green Chile Sauce mixture on the right side of a warm, pliable flour tortilla. Sprinkle 1 tablespoon of grated cheese over the mixture. Fold tortilla in half. Repeat the process with the remaining five flour tortillas; set aside.

Heat a large griddle over high heat until very hot; reduce heat to medium. Place folded tortillas on the hot griddle and brown on both sides for 2 to 3 minutes until the cheese melts. Cut each tortilla into wedges and serve hot immediately.

Serves 6

Each serving provides:

144	Calories	20 g	Carbohydrate
11 g	Protein	391 mg	Sodium
4 g	Fat	22 mg	Cholesterol

35

—✥—

Baked Red Chile Chimichangas

(Chimichangas en Salsa de Chile Rojo)

Preparation time: 25 minutes
Baking time: 10 minutes
Preheat oven to 350°

Many restaurants in the American Southwest offer deep-fried chimichangas. If you like chimichangas but want to avoid the fat and calories, try this recipe. These stuffed tortillas, similar to burritos, are nevertheless just as tasty and nutritious when baked and smothered in a zesty red sauce. For a satisfying low-cal variation of this recipe, prepare the chimichangas with Green Chile Sauce (#15) and extra-lean chicken.

6 fresh lowfat flour tortillas (6-inch)
nonstick pan coating
$\frac{1}{2}$ pound extra-lean round steak, cut into
    1-inch cubes
$\frac{1}{2}$ cup white onions, finely sliced
1 to 2 cloves garlic, crushed in a garlic press
1 fresh anaheim chile, seeded, washed and
    finely chopped
$\frac{1}{8}$ to 1 fresh serrano or jalapeño chile, seeded,
    washed and finely chopped (optional, for
    a spicier dish)
1 small ripe tomato, finely chopped
$1\frac{1}{4}$ cups Red Chile Sauce (Recipe #16)

½ cup green onions, finely sliced
6 sprigs fresh cilantro
salt and freshly ground pepper

Wrap the flour tortillas in foil. Warm in preheated oven for 5 minutes until the tortillas are soft and pliable. Remove from the oven and keep them warm wrapped in the foil; set aside. Evenly spray a baking sheet with non-stick pan coating.

Sauté the meat, white onions, garlic, and anaheim and serrano chiles in a large skillet over medium-high heat until the meat browns evenly on each side; turn frequently. Stir in the tomato and ½ cup of the Red Chile Sauce; reduce heat to low. Simmer the onion and meat mixture for 2 minutes; remove skillet from heat. Salt and pepper to taste.

Evenly spread one-sixth portion of the sautéed onion and meat mixture in the middle of each flour tortilla. Roll each tortilla around the filling in a cylinder shape. Place the rolled chimichangas, seam side down, on the prepared baking sheet. Cover each chimichanga with 2 tablespoons of the remaining Red Chile Sauce. Bake the dish in pre-heated oven for 10 minutes. Remove the chimichangas from oven and place on individual oven-warmed plates. Evenly sprinkle an equal portion of green onions across the top of each chimichanga. Garnish each plate with fresh cilantro sprigs. Serve the hot dish immediately.

Serves 6

Each serving provides:

157	Calories	21 g	Carbohydrate
14 g	Protein	315 mg	Sodium
3 g	Fat	26 mg	Cholesterol

36

❧

Green Enchiladas
with Chicken

(Enchiladas Verdes de Pollo)

Preparation time: 25 minutes
Baking time: 25 minutes

There is more to this succulent dish than meets the eye. It
is a delightful surprise. You will enjoy the unique, zesty
nature of the tart-flavored tomatillo sauce. After eating
these spicy green enchiladas, the sensational flavors linger
hauntingly for hours. For an elegant and appealing dinner,
add Mexican Rice (#52) and a small salad to fully complement this healthful, appetizing enchilada dish.

1 fresh anaheim chile
6 fresh corn tortillas
$1/2$ cup extra-lean chicken, skinned, boned, cooked,
    and coarsely shredded
1 clove garlic, crushed in a garlic press
$1/2$ cup white onions, finely chopped
$1/2$ cup green onions, finely sliced
$1/8$ to 1 fresh serrano or jalapeño chile, seeded, washed,
    and finely chopped (optional, for a spicier dish)
2 cups Tomatillo Sauce (Recipe #18)
$1/3$ cup lowfat Jack cheese, shredded
salt and freshly ground pepper

Preheat the broiler. Roast the anaheim chile 2 to 3 inches
under the broiler for 3 to 4 minutes on each side.
Occasionally rotate the chile until it evenly browns and

blisters on each side. Put the chile in a tightly closed plastic bag to steam for 5 minutes. Carefully peel off the charred skin. Cut off the stem, seed, rinse, and finely chop; set aside.

Wrap the corn tortillas in foil. Warm the tortillas in preheated oven for 10 minutes until the corn tortillas are soft and pliable. Remove tortillas from the oven and keep them warm wrapped in the foil; set aside.

Combine the chicken, garlic, white and green onions, serrano chile and ½ cup of the Tomatillo Sauce in a medium-size bowl. Salt and pepper the mixture according to individual taste. Heat the remaining Tomatillo Sauce over medium-high heat in a small skillet to just below the boiling point; reduce heat to medium-low.

Dip the corn tortillas, one at a time, into the heated sauce. Turn over the corn tortilla and lift out when limp (only 2 to 3 seconds total). Lay each tortilla flat on a small plate. Spoon about ¼ cup of the chicken and onion mixture down the center of each tortilla. Roll up each tortilla and place them side by side, seam side down, in a 9- by 13-inch ungreased, glass baking dish. Evenly spread the remaining Tomatillo Sauce followed by the remaining chicken mixture over the top of the rolled tortillas. Cover the enchiladas with foil. Bake covered in a 350° oven for 15 minutes. Remove enchiladas from oven and evenly sprinkle cheese over the top of the entire dish. Continue baking uncovered for 10 minutes until cheese has melted. Let enchiladas stand 5 minutes before serving.

Serves 6

Each serving provides:

141	Calories	22 g	Carbohydrate
14 g	Protein	158 mg	Sodium
3 g	Fat	26 mg	Cholesterol

37

— ❧ —

Enchilada Pie
(Pastel de Enchiladas)

Preparation time: 20 minutes
Baking time: 15 minutes
Preheat oven to 350°

Different from the more typical enchilada combination, this stacked tortilla dish offers an appealing and easy-to-prepare meal. Enchilada lovers will enjoy this new and easy way to eat enchiladas without any fuss. The spicy beef and red sauce subtly blend with the aromatic flavor of the corn tortillas. Serve this dish with a crisp dinner salad to complement your dinner and make an entire, satisfying meal.

nonstick pan coating
1/2 pound extra-lean ground round
1 medium white onion, chopped
3/4 cup green onions, chopped
1 to 2 cloves garlic, crushed in a garlic press
1 1/2 cups mushrooms, finely sliced
2 cups Mexican Tomato Sauce (Recipe #17)
1/4 teaspoon cumin
2 sprigs fresh cilantro, minced
3 fresh corn tortillas
1/2 cup lowfat Jack cheese, grated
salt and freshly ground pepper

Evenly spray a 10-inch glass pie pan (bake-proof) with nonstick pan coating, entirely covering the bottom so tortillas will not stick to the pan; set aside.

Brown the meat in a large skillet over medium-high

heat until the meat has evenly browned; turn frequently. Drain off any excess fat. Add the white onion, ¹/₂ cup of the green onions, garlic, and mushrooms. Sauté the mixture until the onions become tender; reduce heat to low. Cook the meat and onion mixture for 3 minutes; stir occasionally. Add the Mexican Tomato Sauce, cumin, and cilantro; cook for 2 minutes. Salt and pepper the dish according to individual taste.

Lay 2 tortillas overlapped flatly on the bottom of the prepared glass pie pan. Spread one-half portion of the sautéed meat and onion mixture to cover the tortillas. Lay the remaining tortilla over the top of the enchilada pie. Spread remaining meat and onion mixture over the top tortilla. Sprinkle the top of the enchilada pie with grated jack cheese. Bake in preheated oven for 15 minutes until the meat is thoroughly cooked and cheese has melted. Cut the enchilada pie into wedges and serve garnished with the remaining green onions. Serve the hot enchilada pie immediately.

Serves 6

Each serving provides:

179	Calories	13 g	Carbohydrate
19 g	Protein	191 mg	Sodium
6 g	Fat	40 mg	Cholesterol

38

— ❧ —

Cottage Cheese Enchiladas
(Enchiladas de Requesón)

Preparation time: 25 minutes
Baking time: 20 minutes

This is a variation on the popular enchilada dish which is
equally nutritious and appealing. Cottage cheese adds a
new twist to this classic Mexican dish. Lovers of cottage
cheese will agree that this combination of spicy and appetizing ingredients is a natural hit. Don't forget to use
fresh, soft tortillas made without lard.

1 fresh anaheim chile
6 fresh corn tortillas
$1/2$ cup nonfat, small-curd cottage cheese
$1/2$ cup white onions, finely chopped
$1/2$ cup green onions, finely sliced
1 clove garlic, crushed in a garlic press
$1/8$ to 1 fresh serrano or jalapeño chile, seeded,
      washed, and finely chopped (optional, for
      a spicier dish)
2 cups Red Chile Sauce (Recipe #16)
$1/4$ teaspoon cumin
$1/3$ cup lowfat Jack cheese, shredded
salt and freshly ground pepper

Preheat the broiler. Roast the anaheim chile 2 to 3 inches
under the broiler for 3 to 4 minutes on each side. Occasionally rotate the chile until it evenly browns and blisters
on each side. Put the chile in a tightly closed plastic bag
to steam for 5 minutes. Carefully peel off the charred

skin. Cut off the stem, seed, rinse, and cut the chile into six 6-inch-long strips; set aside.

Wrap corn tortillas in foil. Warm in preheated oven for 10 minutes until the tortillas are soft and pliable. Remove from oven and keep them warm wrapped in the foil; set aside.

Combine the cottage cheese, white and green onions, garlic, serrano chile, and ½ cup of the Red Chile Sauce in a medium-size bowl. Salt and pepper the mixture according to individual taste. Heat the remaining Red Chile Sauce and cumin over medium-high heat in a small skillet to just before the boiling point.

Dip the corn tortillas, one at a time, into the heated sauce. Turn over the corn tortilla and lift out when limp (2 to 3 seconds total). Lay each corn tortilla flat on a dish. Evenly spread about ¼ cup of the cottage cheese and onion mixture down the center of each corn tortilla and top with 1 anaheim chile strip. Roll up each tortilla and place side by side, seam side down, in a 9- by 13-inch ungreased, glass baking dish. Spoon the remaining Red Chile Sauce followed by the remaining cottage cheese and onion mixture over the top of the tortillas. Evenly sprinkle cheese over the entire enchilada dish. Bake uncovered in a 350° oven for 20 minutes. Let the enchiladas stand 5 minutes before serving.

Serves 6

Each serving provides:			
122	Calories	15 g	Carbohydrate
8 g	Protein	216 mg	Sodium
3 g	Fat	11 mg	Cholesterol

39

—❦—

Beef Enchiladas

(Enchiladas de Carne)

Preparation time: 25 minutes
Baking time: 20 minutes

Here is another fashionable enchilada variation. These
enchiladas combine the appetizing flavors of a rich-tasting
red sauce with beef and chiles. You can prepare this elegant enchilada dish in advance and store it in the refrigerator to bake at a later time. Serve enchiladas with a side
dish of fruit for a light and luscious lunch. For a larger,
delicious meal, serve the enchiladas with a crisp dinner
salad and Mexican Rice (#52).

1 fresh anaheim chile
6 fresh corn tortillas
$^1/_2$ cup white onions, finely chopped
$^1/_2$ cup green onions, finely sliced
1 clove garlic, crushed in a garlic press
$^1/_8$ to 1 fresh serrano or jalapeño chile, seeded,
    washed, and finely chopped (optional, for a
    spicier dish)
1 cup extra-lean round steak, cooked and shredded
2 cups Red Chile Sauce (Recipe #16)
$^1/_3$ cup lowfat Jack cheese, grated
salt and freshly ground pepper

Preheat the broiler. Roast anaheim chile 2 to 3 inches
under the broiler for 3 to 4 minutes on each side.
Occasionally rotate the chile until it evenly browns and
blisters on each side. Put the chile in a tightly closed plastic

bag to steam for 5 minutes. Carefully peel off the charred skin. Cut off the stem, seed, rinse, and coarsely chop the chile; set aside.

Wrap the corn tortillas in foil. Warm the tortillas in preheated oven for 10 minutes until soft. Remove tortillas from oven and keep them warm wrapped in the foil; set aside.

Combine the white and green onions, garlic, anaheim and serrano chiles, beef, and ½ cup of the Red Chile Sauce in a medium-size bowl. Salt and pepper the mixture according to individual taste. Heat the remaining Red Chile Sauce over medium-high heat in a small skillet to just before the boiling point.

Dip the warm corn tortillas, one at a time, into the heated sauce. Turn over the corn tortilla and lift out when limp (2 to 3 seconds total). Lay each corn tortilla flat on a dish. Evenly spread about ¼ cup of the onion and beef mixture down the center of each corn tortilla. Roll up each tortilla and place side by side, seam side down, in a 9- by 13-inch ungreased, glass baking pan. Spoon the remaining Red Chile Sauce followed by the remaining onion and beef mixture over the top of the corn tortillas. Evenly sprinkle grated Jack cheese over the entire dish of enchiladas. Bake uncovered in 350° oven for 20 minutes until the cheese is melted. Let the enchiladas stand 5 minutes before serving.

Serves 6

Each serving provides:

174	Calories	14 g	Carbohydrate
17 g	Protein	148 mg	Sodium
4 g	Fat	36 mg	Cholesterol

40

❧

Chicken Enchiladas
(Enchiladas de Pollo)

Preparation time: 25 minutes
Baking time: 20 minutes

Instead of rolling the tortillas, fold the tortillas in half and
layer the enchiladas against each other for an eye-appealing
adaptation of the classic Mexican enchilada dish. The corn
tortillas, chicken, and spicy Red Chile Sauce are an unbeatable combination for healthful and savory flavors. Serve
these enchiladas with a portion of beans and a garden-fresh
salad for a delicious, appetizing meal.

1 fresh anaheim chile
6 fresh corn tortillas
1/2 cup white onions, finely chopped
1/2 cup green onions, finely sliced
1 clove garlic, crushed in a garlic press
1/8 to 1 fresh serrano or jalapeño chile, seeded,
    washed, and finely chopped (optional, for a
    spicier dish)
1 cup extra-lean chicken, skinned, boned, cooked,
    and shredded
2 cups Red Chile Sauce (Recipe #16)
6 tablespoons lowfat Jack cheese, grated
salt and freshly ground pepper

Preheat the broiler. Roast the anaheim chile 2 to 3 inches
under the broiler for 3 to 4 minutes on each side.
Occasionally rotate the chile until it evenly browns and
blisters on each side. Put the chile in a tightly closed plastic

bag to steam for 5 minutes. Carefully peel off the charred skin. Cut off the stem, seed, rinse, and coarsely chop the chile; set aside.

Wrap the corn tortillas in foil. Warm in preheated oven for 5 minutes until tortillas are soft. Remove from oven and keep them warm wrapped in the foil; set aside.

Combine the white and green onions, garlic, anaheim and serrano chiles, chicken, and ½ cup of the Red Chile Sauce in a medium-size bowl. Salt and pepper the mixture according to individual taste. Heat the remaining Red Chile Sauce over medium-high heat in a small skillet to just before the boiling point.

Dip the corn tortillas, one at a time, into the heated sauce. Turn over the corn tortilla and lift out when limp (2 to 3 seconds total). Lay each corn tortilla flat on a dish. Evenly spread about ¼ cup of the onion and chicken mixture down the center of each tortilla. Fill and fold the next corn tortilla in half and layer the enchiladas side by side, half on top of each other, in a 9- by 13-inch ungreased, glass baking dish. Continue filling and folding the next four tortillas. Spoon the remaining Red Chile Sauce followed by the onion and chicken mixture over the top of the tortillas. Evenly sprinkle grated jack cheese over the entire dish of enchiladas. Bake uncovered in a 350° oven for 20 minutes. Let the enchiladas stand 5 minutes before serving.

Serves 6

Each serving provides:

162	Calories	25 g	Carbohydrate
20 g	Protein	152 mg	Sodium
3 g	Fat	42 mg	Cholesterol

41

Swiss Enchiladas

(Enchiladas Suizas)

Preparation time: 25 minutes
Baking time: 20 minutes

This cheese-filled enchilada dish offers a scintillating combination of swiss cheese, corn tortillas, and chiles. Popular both in Mexico and America, this recipe is lower in fat and calories than most. For a satisfying dinner, complement this dish with a side dish of vegetables or rice and a garden-fresh dinner salad.

1 fresh anaheim chile
6 fresh corn tortillas
½ cup white onions, finely chopped
½ cup green onions, finely sliced
1 clove garlic, crushed in a garlic press
⅛ to 1 fresh serrano or jalapeño chile, seeded,
    washed, and finely chopped (optional, for
    a spicier dish)
2 cups Green Chile Sauce (Recipe #15)
1 cup lowfat swiss cheese, grated
salt and freshly ground pepper

Preheat the broiler. Roast the anaheim chile 2 to 3 inches under the broiler for 3 to 4 minutes on each side. Occasionally rotate the chile until it evenly browns and blisters on each side. Put the chile in a tightly closed plastic bag to steam for 5 minutes. Carefully peel off the charred skin. Cut off the stem, seed, rinse, and cut the chile into six strips; set aside.

Wrap the corn tortillas in foil. Warm in preheated oven for 10 minutes until the tortillas are soft. Remove from oven and keep them warm wrapped in the foil; set aside.

Combine the white and green onions, garlic, serrano chile, 1/2 cup of the Green Chile Sauce, and 2/3 cup of the grated cheese in a medium-size bowl. Salt and pepper the mixture according to individual taste. Heat the remaining Green Chile Sauce over medium-high heat in a small skillet to just before the boiling point.

Dip the corn tortillas, one at a time, into the heated sauce. Turn over the corn tortilla and lift out when limp (2 to 3 seconds total). Lay each corn tortilla flat on a dish. Evenly spread about 1/4 cup of the onion and cheese mixture down the center of each tortilla. Lay one strip of anaheim chile across the top. Roll up each corn tortilla and place side by side, seam side down, in a 9- by 13-inch ungreased, glass baking dish. Spoon the remaining Green Chile Sauce followed by the onion and cheese mixture over the top of the tortillas. Evenly sprinkle the remaining swiss cheese over the entire dish. Bake the enchilada dish uncovered in a 350° oven for 20 minutes. Let the enchiladas stand 5 minutes before serving.

Serves 6

Each serving provides:

190	Calories	15 g	Carbohydrate
14 g	Protein	324 mg	Sodium
8 g	Fat	30 mg	Cholesterol

42

—✤—

Shrimp Enchiladas

(Enchiladas de Camarón)

Preparation time: 20 minutes
Baking time: 20 minutes

These attractive, low-calorie enchiladas will delight
seafood fans with the blended flavor of shrimp, corn, and
Green Chile Sauce. Be sure that the shrimp is fresh and
bright pink when you fill the enchiladas. Serve smaller
portions cut in slices, garnished with coriander and lime
wedges, as a great appetizer for an elegant, formal dinner
for guests.

1 fresh anaheim chile
6 fresh corn tortillas
$3/4$ cup large raw shrimp, peeled, deveined, and
　　coarsely chopped
$1/2$ cup white onions, finely chopped
$1/2$ cup green onions, finely sliced
1 clove garlic, crushed in a garlic press
$1/8$ to 1 fresh serrano or jalapeño chile, seeded,
　　washed, and finely chopped (optional, for a
　　spicier dish)
2 cups Green Chile Sauce (Recipe #15)
$1/3$ cup lowfat Jack cheese, grated
salt and freshly ground pepper

Preheat the broiler. Roast the anaheim chile 2 to 3 inches
under the broiler for 3 to 4 minutes on each side. Occasionally rotate the chile until it evenly browns and blisters
on all sides. Put the chile in a tightly closed plastic bag to

steam for 5 minutes. Carefully peel off the charred skin. Cut off the stem, seed, rinse, and finely chop; set aside.

Wrap the corn tortillas in foil. Warm in preheated oven for 10 minutes until soft. Remove the tortillas from the oven and keep them warm wrapped in the foil; set aside.

Cook the shrimp in 3 cups of water for 4 minutes until the shrimp turn pink; drain and set aside. Combine the white and green onions, garlic, anaheim and serrano chiles, cooked shrimp, and 1/2 cup of the Green Chile Sauce in a medium-size bowl. Salt and pepper the mixture according to individual taste. Heat the remaining Green Chile Sauce over medium-high heat in a small skillet to just before the boiling point.

Dip the corn tortillas, one at a time, into the heated sauce. Turn over the corn tortilla and lift out when limp (2 to 3 seconds total). Lay each tortilla flat on a dish. Evenly spread about 1/6 cup of the onion and shrimp mixture down the center of each tortilla. Roll up each corn tortilla and place side by side, seam side down, in a 9- by 13-inch ungreased, glass baking dish. Spoon the remaining Green Chile Sauce and the remaining onion and shrimp mixture over the top of the tortillas. Evenly sprinkle the Jack cheese over the entire dish. Bake uncovered in a 350° oven for 20 minutes. Let the enchilada dish stand 5 minutes before serving.

Serves 6

Each serving provides:

140	Calories	15 g	Carbohydrate
12 g	Protein	186 mg	Sodium
3 g	Fat	53 mg	Cholesterol

43

❧

Soft Chicken Tacos

(Tacos de Pollo)

Preparation time: 20 minutes
Preheat oven to 350°

Here is a low-calorie twist to the classic Mexican taco;
this is not a fried taco recipe. You can eat these soft tacos,
made with flour instead of corn tortillas, alone for a light,
appetizing lunch. Add a side dish of beans or rice and a
garden-fresh salad for a festive and satisfying dinner.
Easy to prepare and delicious, you will welcome the
chance to regularly enjoy the popular taco stuffed with
appetizing ingredients. Serve the tacos with a bowl of
salsa on the side. As an alternative, you might like to substitute the chicken with beef, pork, or turkey.

6 fresh lowfat flour tortillas (6-inch)
$^1/_2$ cup white onions, finely chopped
$^1/_2$ cup green onions, finely sliced
1 clove garlic, crushed in a garlic press
1 fresh anaheim chile, seeded, washed, and
    finely chopped
$^1/_8$ to 1 fresh serrano or jalapeño chile, seeded, washed,
    and finely chopped (optional, for a spicier dish)
$^1/_2$ cup extra-lean chicken, skinned, boned, cooked,
    and shredded
$^1/_3$ cup Red Chile Sauce (Recipe #16)
$^1/_4$ teaspoon fresh oregano, minced
$^3/_4$ cup lettuce, shredded
$^1/_2$ small ripe tomato, finely chopped
salt and freshly ground pepper

Wrap the flour tortillas in foil. Warm in preheated oven for 5 minutes until the tortillas are soft and pliable. Remove from oven and keep them warm wrapped in the foil; set aside.

Sauté the white and green onions, garlic, and anaheim and serrano chiles with 2 tablespoons of water in a large skillet over medium-high heat until the onions become tender; stir frequently. Add the chicken, Red Chile Sauce, and oregano; reduce heat to low. Simmer the onion and chicken mixture uncovered, stirring occasionally, for 2 minutes. Salt and pepper the chicken mixture according to individual taste.

Remove skillet from burner. Evenly spread one-sixth portion of the onion and chicken mixture on the right side of each flour tortilla. Add one-sixth portion of the lettuce and tomatoes to each tortilla. Fold each tortilla in half and serve immediately.

Serves 6

Each taco provides:

115	Calories	25 g	Carbohydrate
10 g	Protein	316 mg	Sodium
2 g	Fat	16 mg	Cholesterol

44

❦

Soft Vegetable Tacos

(Tacos de Verduras)

Preparation time: 20 minutes
Preheat oven to 350°

These soft vegetable tacos are another variation of the
light and lively soft taco. You can fill the versatile flour
tortilla with just about any kind of leftovers. As an alternative, you might like to substitute the vegetables in this
recipe with rice, beans, or other vegetables.

6 fresh lowfat flour tortillas (6-inch)
1 small zucchini, quartered and finely sliced
1/2 cup white onions, finely chopped
1/2 cup green onions, finely sliced
1 fresh anaheim chile, seeded, washed,
        and finely chopped
1 cup mushrooms, finely sliced
1/3 cup Mexican Tomato Sauce (Recipe #17)
1 clove garlic, crushed in a garlic press
1 teaspoon fresh oregano, minced
1 teaspoon fresh thyme, minced
3/4 cup lettuce, shredded
1 small ripe tomato, finely chopped
6 sprigs fresh cilantro
salt and freshly ground pepper

Wrap the flour tortillas in foil. Warm in preheated oven
for 5 minutes until tortillas are soft. Remove from oven
and keep warm wrapped in the foil; set aside.

Place a steamer basket inside a 5-quart pot. Bring 1 inch of water in the pot to the boiling point; reduce heat to low. Set the zucchini in the pot on the steamer basket. Cook the zucchini, partially covered, about 5 minutes. Add the white and green onions, anaheim chile, and mushrooms to the pot. Cook the vegetables, partially covered, for 3 to 4 minutes until just tender; drain. Heat the Mexican Tomato Sauce, garlic, oregano, and thyme over medium heat in a small saucepan for 2 minutes. Stir in the hot, steamed vegetables. Salt and pepper the vegetable and Mexican Tomato Sauce mixture according to individual taste.

Evenly spread one-sixth portion of the vegetable mixture on the right side of each flour tortilla. Add one-sixth portion of the lettuce, tomato, and cilantro to each tortilla. Fold each tortilla in half and serve immediately.

Serves 6

Each taco provides:

97	Calories	22 g	Carbohydrate
3 g	Protein	303 mg	Sodium
1 g	Fat	0 mg	Cholesterol

45

❦

Chicken Tostadas
(Tostadas de Pollo)

Preparation time: 20 minutes
Preheat oven to 350°

Chicken tostadas offer the nutritious, appealing combination of spicy and delicious fresh ingredients. The corn tortillas are baked instead of fried to reduce the amount of fat and calories. Serve chicken tostadas alone for a light lunch or add rice for a satisfying and delicious dinner. Use leftover grilled chicken, beef, vegetables, or other appetizing choices as an alternative to this festive and easy-to-prepare dish.

6 fresh corn tortillas
1 small white onion, finely chopped
½ cup green onions, finely sliced
1 to 2 cloves garlic, crushed in a garlic press
1 fresh anaheim chile, seeded, washed, and
    finely chopped
1 cup extra-lean chicken, skinned, boned, cooked,
    and cut into 1-inch cubes
1½ cups Mexican Tomato Sauce (Recipe #17)
3 cups iceberg lettuce, shredded
1 small tomato, finely chopped
salt and freshly ground pepper

Place the corn tortillas flat on a large baking sheet. Warm in preheated oven for 10 minutes. Wrap the tortillas in foil to keep them warm; set aside.

Sauté the white onion, ¹/₄ cup of the green onions, garlic, and anaheim chile with 2 tablespoons of water in a skillet over medium-high heat until the onions become tender; stir frequently. Add the chicken and 1 cup of Mexican Tomato Sauce. Salt and pepper the onion and chicken mixture according to individual taste.

Arrange the corn tortillas on six oven-warmed plates. Use a slotted spoon to spread one-sixth portion of the onion and chicken mixture on each tortilla. Cover with one-sixth portion of the lettuce and tomato. Spoon the remaining Mexican Tomato Sauce over the top of each tostada. Garnish the tostadas with the remaining green onions.

Serves 6

Each tostada provides:

133	Calories	27 g	Carbohydrate
17 g	Protein	66 mg	Sodium
1 g	Fat	32 mg	Cholesterol

46

❦

Bean Tostadas

(Tostadas de Frijoles)

Preparation time: 15 minutes
Preheat oven to 350°

Reminiscent of the original healthful Indian diet, these quick and easy-to-prepare bean tostadas offer the nutritious combination of corn, beans, and chiles. The corn tortillas are baked instead of fried to reduce the amount of fat and calories. Serve bean tostadas alone for a light lunch or add a side dish of rice for a satisfying and delicious dinner.

2 corn tortillas
$1/4$ cup white onions, finely chopped
1 clove garlic, crushed in a garlic press
$1/2$ fresh anaheim chile, seeded, washed, and
    finely chopped
$1/8$ to 1 fresh serrano or jalapeño chile, seeded, washed,
    and finely chopped (optional, for a spicier dish)
$1/2$ cup pinto beans, cooked and mashed
2 to 4 sprigs fresh cilantro, minced (optional)
$1/2$ cup Mexican Tomato Sauce (Recipe #17)
2 cups iceberg lettuce, shredded
$1/4$ cup tomato, finely chopped
2 tablespoons green onions, finely sliced
salt and freshly ground pepper

Place the tortillas flat on a large baking sheet. Warm in preheated oven for 10 minutes. Wrap the tortillas in foil to keep them warm; set aside.

Sauté the white onions, garlic, and anaheim and serrano chiles with 1 tablespoon of water in a small skillet over medium-high heat until the onions become tender; stir frequently. Stir in the mashed pinto beans, cilantro, and ¼ cup of the Mexican Tomato Sauce; reduce heat to low. Salt and pepper the dish according to individual taste.

Arrange the corn tortillas on two oven-warmed plates. Spread one-half portion of the sautéed onion and bean mixture on each tortilla. Cover the beans on each tostada with 1 cup lettuce, 2 tablespoons tomato, 1 tablespoon green onions, and the remaining Mexican Tomato Sauce. Serve the tostadas immediately.

Serves 2

Each tostada provides:

159	Calories	29 g	Carbohydrate
8 g	Protein	75 mg	Sodium
1 g	Fat	0 mg	Cholesterol

47

—❧—

Tortillas Soaked in Green Sauce

(Chilaquiles en Salsa Verde)

Preparation time: 15 minutes
Baking time: 15 minutes

This popular Mexican dish is the ideal way to use up old
tortillas. The tortilla pieces soak up the spicy, blended
juices of the Green Chile Sauce, tomatoes, and herbs.
These ingredients will pleasantly fill your kitchen with
earthy, tantalizing aromas. Serve this colorful and savory
dish with a festive salad, rice, or beans.

nonstick pan coating
1 fresh lowfat flour tortilla (6-inch)
2 fresh lowfat corn tortillas
2 fresh anaheim chiles
1 medium white onion, finely chopped
$1/2$ cup green onions, finely sliced
1 clove garlic, crushed in a garlic press
$1/8$ to 1 fresh serrano or jalapeño chile, minced
      (optional, for a spicier dish)
2 medium ripe tomatoes, blanched or roasted,
      peeled, and finely chopped
2 cups Green Chile Sauce (Recipe #15)
2 to 4 sprigs fresh cilantro, minced
$1/3$ cup lowfat Jack cheese, grated
salt and freshly ground pepper

Evenly spray a glass baking dish with nonstick pan coating, entirely covering the bottom so tortillas will not stick; set aside. Cut the flour and corn tortillas in half and then cut into strips approximately ½-inch wide. Lay the tortilla strips across a baking sheet and bake in preheated oven for 10 minutes until crisp; set aside.

Preheat the broiler. Roast the anaheim chiles 2 to 3 inches under the broiler for 3 to 4 minutes on each side. Occasionally rotate the chiles until they evenly brown and blister on each side. Put chiles in a tightly closed plastic bag to steam for 5 minutes. Carefully peel off the charred skin. Cut off the stem, seed, rinse, and finely chop.

Sauté the white and green onions, garlic, and anaheim and serrano chiles with 2 tablespoons of water in a medium-size saucepan over medium-high heat until the onions become tender; stir frequently. Add the tomatoes; cook mixture for 2 minutes. Add the Green Chile Sauce and minced cilantro; reduce heat to low. Salt and pepper to taste.

Evenly spread one-half portion of the baked tortilla strips on the bottom of the prepared baking dish. Add a layer of one-half portion of the onion and Green Chile Sauce mixture. Repeat process until you have used the remaining tortillas and onion and Green Chile Sauce mixture. Evenly sprinkle Jack cheese across the top. Bake uncovered in a 350° oven for 15 minutes until cheese has thoroughly melted. Cut the *chilaquiles* into squares and serve hot.

Serves 6

Each serving provides:

108	Calories	15 g	Carbohydrate
6 g	Protein	168 mg	Sodium
3 g	Fat	10 mg	Cholesterol

48

—❧—

Red Chile Burritos

(Burritos Rojos)

Preparation time: 30 minutes
Preheat oven at 350°

Try this mouth-watering combination of spicy, red chile
sauce and beef stuffed in a fresh, warm tortilla. As a delicious alternative, substitute the beef with pork, chicken,
or turkey. If you like, cut the burritos into small slices and
serve them as a great appetizer before an elegant dinner
for guests. To create a festive, satisfying dinner, serve
these burritos with a vegetable dish, rice, or vermicelli.

6 fresh lowfat flour tortillas (7-inch)
2½ cups Red Chile Sauce (Recipe #16)
½ pound extra-lean round steak, cut into
    1-inch cubes
1 medium white onion, finely sliced
¾ cup green onions, finely sliced
1 to 2 cloves garlic, crushed in a garlic press
⅛ to 1 fresh serrano or jalapeño chile, seeded, washed
    and finely chopped (optional, for a spicier dish)
1 fresh anaheim chile, seeded, washed,
    and finely chopped
1 small-size ripe tomato, finely chopped
6 sprigs fresh cilantro, minced
salt and freshly ground pepper

Wrap the flour tortillas in foil. Warm in preheated oven
for 10 minutes until the tortillas are soft and pliable.

Remove from oven and keep them warm wrapped in the foil; set aside.

Warm 2 cups of the Red Chile Sauce over low heat in a small saucepan. Heat a large skillet over medium-high heat. Evenly brown the meat to sear in the juices; stir frequently. Add the white onion and ½ cup of the green onions, garlic, and serrano and anaheim chiles. Sauté the onion and meat mixture until the onions become tender; stir frequently. Add the tomato; reduce heat to low. Simmer the onion and meat mixture uncovered, stirring occasionally, for 2 minutes. Stir in the remaining ½ cup of the Red Chile Sauce.

Use a slotted spoon to evenly spread one-sixth portion of the onion and meat mixture in the middle of each warmed flour tortilla. Roll each tortilla around the filling in a cylinder shape. Place the rolled burritos, seam side down, on oven-warmed plates. Cover each burrito with one-sixth portion of the remaining warmed Red Chile Sauce in the saucepan. Evenly sprinkle the top of each burrito with the remaining green onions. Garnish each plate with minced cilantro sprigs. Serve the hot burritos immediately.

Serves 6

Each burrito provides:

173	Calories	24 g	Carbohydrate
14 g	Protein	64 mg	Sodium
3 g	Fat	26 mg	Cholesterol

49

—✤—

Green Chile Burritos

(Burritos Verdes)

Preparation time: 30 minutes
Preheat oven at 350°

A savory green chile sauce and chicken are an unbeatable combination when stuffed in a fresh, warm tortilla. As an alternative, substitute the chicken with pork, beef, or turkey. If you like, cut the burritos into small slices and surprise your guests with an appealing appetizer before an elegant dinner. For a pleasing meal, serve these burritos with a vegetable dish, rice, or vermicelli.

6 fresh lowfat flour tortillas (6-inch)
2$^{1}/_{2}$ cups Green Chile Sauce (Recipe #15)
$^{1}/_{2}$ pound extra-lean chicken, skinned, boned,
    and cut into 1$^{1}/_{2}$-inch cubes
1 medium white onion, finely sliced
$^{3}/_{4}$ cup green onions, finely sliced
1 to 2 cloves garlic, crushed in a garlic press
$^{1}/_{8}$ to 1 fresh serrano or jalapeño chile, seeded,
    washed, and finely chopped (optional, for
    a spicier dish)
1 fresh anaheim chile, seeded, washed,
    and finely chopped
6 sprigs fresh cilantro
salt and freshly ground pepper

Wrap the flour tortillas in foil. Warm in preheated oven for 10 minutes until soft and pliable. Remove from the oven and keep them warm wrapped in the foil; set aside.

Warm 2 cups of the Green Chile Sauce over low heat in a small saucepan. Heat a large skillet over medium-high heat. Evenly brown the chicken to sear in the juices; stir frequently. Add the white onion and ½ cup of the green onions, garlic, and serrano and anaheim chiles. Sauté the onion and chicken mixture until the onions become tender; stir frequently. Stir in remaining ½ cup of the Green Chile Sauce. Simmer the onion and chicken mixture for 2 minutes; remove skillet from heat. Salt and pepper to taste.

Evenly spread one-sixth portion of the onion and chicken mixture in the middle of each flour tortilla. Roll each tortilla around the filling in a cylinder shape. Place the rolled burritos, seam side down, on oven-warmed plates. Cover each burrito with one-sixth portion of the remaining Green Chile Sauce in the saucepan. Evenly sprinkle the top of each burrito with remaining green onions. Garnish each plate with fresh cilantro sprigs. Serve the hot dish immediately.

Serves 6

Each burrito provides:

155	Calories	34 g	Carbohydrate
17 g	Protein	79 mg	Sodium
2 g	Fat	32 mg	Cholesterol

50

❦

Mexican-style Pizza
(Pizza a la Mexicana)

Preparation time: 15 minutes
Preheat oven at 350°

This is an easily prepared appetizer, lunch, or late-night snack for two hungry pizza lovers. For an equally satisfying alternative, try chicken and Red Chile Sauce (#16) in this recipe. This recipe is so easy, you can always quickly make this tantalizing treat in time for the next football or basketball game on television.

2 fresh lowfat flour tortillas (6-inch)
1/4 cup white onions, finely chopped
1/4 cup green onions, finely sliced
1 clove garlic, crushed in a garlic press
1/2 fresh anaheim chile, finely chopped and seeded
1/4 cup mushrooms, finely chopped
2 tablespoons Mexican Tomato Sauce (Recipe #17)
1/4 cup lowfat jack cheese, grated
salt and freshly ground pepper

Wrap the flour tortillas in foil. Warm in preheated oven for 5 minutes until soft and pliable.

Sauté the white and green onions, garlic, anaheim chile, and mushrooms with 2 tablespoons of water in a medium-size skillet over medium-high heat until the chiles and onions become tender; stir frequently. Add the Mexican Tomato Sauce to the onion and mushroom mixture; reduce heat to low. Cook the onion and mushroom mixture for 2 minutes; stir occasionally. Salt and pepper the dish according to individual taste.

Heat a griddle over medium-high until hot. Lay a flour tortilla flat on the hot griddle. Use a slotted spoon to evenly spread one-half portion of the onion and mushroom mixture on the flour tortilla. Gently spread the mixture to the sides of the tortilla. Sprinkle 2 tablespoons of the grated cheese over the flour tortilla. Cook 3 minutes until cheese melts. Repeat the same process with the second tortilla. Cut the Mexican-style pizza into four wedges and serve hot immediately.

Serves 4

Each serving provides:

88	Calories	11 g	Carbohydrate
6 g	Protein	131 mg	Sodium
3 g	Fat	10 mg	Cholesterol

Mexican Vegetable and Grain Dishes

Nutritionists often write about the important nutritional value of vegetables and grains. Typically high in vitamins, fibers, and minerals, vegetables and grains are low in fat, sodium, and cholesterol. Fresh vegetables and grains are also an important source of carbohydrates. Served with each meal, grains and vegetables provide healthful additions to your choice of any appetizing Mexican meal.

Large, busy open-air markets and American-style supermarkets, brimming with fresh fruits, vegetables, and grains, are popular places to shop in Mexico. Offering a spectacular and intriguing variety of products, these markets display Mexico's rich abundance of fresh vegetable produce and grains. Grains and vegetables are a fundamental part of the nutritious Mexican diet.

It is important that cooks understand the unique process of obtaining balanced protein sources from non-animal protein. Eaten with the right food combination, vegetables and grains are a vital, economical source of protein. Vegetables and grains provide incomplete proteins because they have insufficient amounts of certain essential amino acids. In its solitary state, the body cannot use incomplete proteins to meet daily protein requirements.

Fortunately, different types of complementary vegetables or grains eaten together during the same meal will create a complete protein. Complementary proteins will complement or make up for amino acid deficiencies, if combined. For example, corn is a vegetable that is high in the amino acid methionine but low in the amino acid lysine. Beans are complementary to corn because they are high in lysine but low in methionine. Rice is another example of a rich source of incomplete protein that is complementary with corn. The complete protein found in most animals, such as poultry, beef, or fish, will also successfully complement the incomplete protein found in vegetables and grains. Complementary proteins combined correctly can provide just as much protein as a steak or chicken without the high cholesterol and fat content or calories. Most of the world's cuisine relies on this complementary protein process to meet its nutritional requirements.

Here are three important tips for cooking the best vegetable and grain dishes. Good cooks always use fresh, unblemished vegetables because they are more nutritious than canned or processed products. Remember to wash vegetables thoroughly to rid them of dirt, germs, and unwanted chemicals. Lastly, always cook vegetables and grains as little as possible or until just tender.

The recipes found in *Mexican Vegetable and Grain Dishes* present an assortment of fascinating, easy-to-prepare vegetable and grain dishes. These spicy, versatile dishes are great as a zesty side dish or a one-dish meal. This section offers recipes to use a common variety of fresh vegetables and grains which uniquely blend with spicy chiles. Whatever your special choice, these savory, nutritious vegetable dishes will enhance your home-cooked meals and superbly display your culinary expertise.

Mexican Vegetable
and Grain Dishes

51

❦

Spicy Vermicelli
(Sopa Seca de Fideo)

Preparation time: 10 minutes
Cooking time: 10 to 15 minutes

Noodle lovers will love this appetizing, nutritious dish
blended with the subtle, enticing flavors of tomatoes and
chiles. The translation of the Mexican name for this
unusual and appealing side dish is "dry vermicelli soup."
This dish is not actually a soup but looks soupy when it
begins to cook. The noodles quickly absorb the soupy liquid after cooking. You can serve the vermicelli separately
or as an incomparable side dish for many exciting
Mexican dishes.

½ cup white onions, diced
½ cup green onions, finely sliced
1 to 2 cloves garlic, crushed in a garlic press
⅛ to 1 fresh serrano or jalapeño chile, seeded,
  washed, and chopped (optional, for a
  spicier dish)
4 ounces thin vermicelli noodles, broken into
  3- to 4-inch pieces
1 cup Mexican Tomato Sauce (Recipe #17)
1 cup Red Chile Sauce (Recipe #16)
2½ cups water
2 to 4 sprigs fresh cilantro, minced (optional)
salt and freshly ground pepper

Stirring frequently, sauté the white and green onions, garlic, and serrano chiles with 2 tablespoons of water in a

large skillet over medium-high heat until the white onions become tender; reduce heat to low. Add the vermicelli noodles. Stir in the Mexican Tomato and Red Chile Sauces and water; mix well. Stir the mixture to cover the noodles thoroughly in the liquid. About ½ inch of water should cover the noodles. Cover; cook for 10 to 15 minutes until the noodles become tender and the liquid has been absorbed. Do not let the noodles cook dry. If necessary, add additional hot water, ¼ cup at a time, to avoid burning the noodles. Salt and pepper the dish according to individual taste. Garnish the vermicelli with fresh cilantro before serving.

Serves 6

Each serving provides:

92	Calories	19 g	Carbohydrate
3 g	Protein	13 mg	Sodium
1 g	Fat	0 mg	Cholesterol

52

❧

Mexican Rice

(Arroz a la Mexicana)

Preparation time: 10 minutes
Cooking time: 20 minutes

This popular rice dish is often known as Mexican or
Spanish "dry soup." You will enjoy the tender rice served
separately or as an accompaniment to many special
Mexican dishes, like *chilaquiles,* tacos, or enchiladas.
Originally introduced by the Spaniards, this piquant rice
dish, tomato-bright in color, was quickly assimilated into
the Mexican diet.

nonstick pan coating
³/₄ cup long-grain rice, uncooked
1 small white onion, finely chopped
¹/₂ cup green onions, finely sliced
1 clove garlic, crushed in a garlic press
¹/₂ cup Mexican Tomato Sauce (Recipe #17)
1 cup low-salt broth
1 cup water
salt and freshly ground pepper

Evenly spray a large skillet with nonstick pan coating,
entirely covering the bottom so ingredients will not stick.
Sauté the rice, white and green onions, and garlic over
medium-high heat in the prepared skillet until the rice
lightly browns and the onions become tender; stir frequently. Stir in the remaining ingredients; combine well.
Reduce heat to medium-low. About ¹/₂ inch of water
should cover the rice. Cover; cook about 20 minutes until

the rice becomes tender and entirely absorbs the liquid. Do not let the rice cook dry. If necessary, add additional hot water, $^{1}/_{4}$ cup at a time, to avoid burning the rice. Serve the hot rice immediately. Salt and pepper the dish according to individual taste.

Serves 6

Each serving provides:

76	Calories	20 g	Carbohydrate
2 g	Protein	11 mg	Sodium
0 g	Fat	0 mg	Cholesterol

53

—✥—

Mexican Rice with Vegetables

(Arroz a la Mexicana con Verduras)

Preparation time: 10 minutes
Cooking time: 20 minutes

This wonderfully tasty rice recipe makes a mouth-watering side dish to accompany most Mexican dishes. The vegetables add an attractive, contrasting color and texture to the tomato-bright color of this rice dish. As usual, the tomatoes and chiles add a sensational earthy flavor.

nonstick pan coating
³/₄ cup long-grain rice, uncooked
1 medium white onion, finely chopped
¹/₄ cup green onions, finely sliced
¹/₄ cup carrots, cut into ¹/₂-inch cubes
1 to 2 cloves garlic, crushed in a garlic press
1 fresh anaheim chile, seeded, washed, and
       finely chopped
³/₄ cup Mexican Tomato Sauce (Recipe #17)
1 cup low-salt broth
1¹/₂ cups water
salt and freshly ground pepper

Evenly spray a large skillet with nonstick pan coating, entirely covering the bottom of the skillet so ingredients will not stick. Sauté the rice, white and green onions, and carrots over medium-high heat in the prepared skillet until the rice lightly browns and the onions become tender; stir frequently. Stir in the remaining ingredients; combine well. Reduce heat to low. About ½ inch of water should cover the rice. Cover; cook for 20 minutes until the rice becomes tender and entirely absorbs the liquid. Do not let the rice cook dry. If necessary, add additional hot water, ¼ cup at a time, to avoid burning the rice. Serve the hot rice dish immediately. Salt and pepper the dish according to individual taste.

Serves 8

Each serving provides:

58	Calories	15 g	Carbohydrate
2 g	Protein	14 mg	Sodium
0 g	Fat	0 mg	Cholesterol

54

---✦---

Corn with Chile Strips

(Elote con Rajas)

Preparation time: 10 minutes

The blended flavor of corn and chiles is a savory, nutritious combination and ideal as a side dish for most Mexican meals. The contrast of colors and textures appeals to the discriminating tastes of both cook and guests alike. Use leftovers of this dish as a welcome addition to soups or stews. If you like, serve this tasty dish to complement a healthful, hearty meal with beans, poultry, fish, or beef.

2 large fresh anaheim chiles
$1/8$ to 1 fresh serrano or jalapeño chile, seeded, washed, and finely sliced (optional, for a spicier dish)
1 medium white onion, finely sliced into rings
$1/2$ cup green onions, finely sliced
$1/2$ cup red bell peppers, halved, seeded, and sliced into strips
1 to 2 cloves garlic, crushed in a garlic press
$2^1/2$ cups corn kernels, cooked
salt and freshly ground pepper

Preheat the broiler. Roast the anaheim chiles 2 to 3 inches under the broiler for 3 to 4 minutes on each side. Occasionally rotate the chiles until they evenly brown and blister on each side. Put chiles in a tightly closed plastic bag to steam for 5 minutes. Carefully peel off the charred skin. Cut off the stem, seed, rinse, and cut each chile into strips about $1/2$ inch wide by 3 inches long.

Sauté all the ingredients over medium-high heat in a medium-size saucepan until the onions become tender; reduce heat to low. Cover; cook 4 minutes until the onions become tender. Salt and pepper the dish according to individual taste. Serve the hot corn immediately.

Serves 6

Each serving provides:

91	Calories	21 g	Carbohydrate
3 g	Protein	20 mg	Sodium
1 g	Fat	0 mg	Cholesterol

55

❧

Spicy Garbanzos

(Garbanzos con Rajas)

Preparation time: 15 minutes

This colorful, attractive, high-protein vegetable combination enhances any meal as an appetizing side dish. Homey and easy to prepare, the garbanzo beans are simmered with strips of chiles and onions, called *rajas* in Mexico.

1 fresh anaheim chile
1 small white onion, finely chopped
1/2 cup green onions, finely sliced
1 to 2 cloves garlic, crushed in a garlic press
1/8 to 1 fresh serrano or jalapeño chile, seeded,
 washed, and finely chopped (optional, for a
 spicier dish)
1/2 cup red bell peppers, halved, seeded, washed,
 and sliced into strips
1/2 cup tomato, blanched or roasted, peeled,
 and chopped
1/2 cup Green (Recipe #15) or Red Chile Sauce
 (Recipe #16)
1 1/2 cups garbanzo beans, cooked
2 sprigs cilantro, minced (optional)
salt and freshly ground pepper

Preheat the broiler. Roast the anaheim chile 2 to 3 inches under the broiler for 3 to 4 minutes on each side. Occasionally rotate the chile until it evenly browns and blisters on each side. Put the chile in a tightly closed plastic bag to steam for 5 minutes. Carefully peel off the charred skin. Cut off the stem, seed, rinse, and finely slice the chile into short strips; set aside.

Sauté the white and green onions, garlic, anaheim and serrano chiles, and red bell peppers with 2 tablespoons of water in a medium-size saucepan over medium-high heat until the onions become tender; stir frequently. Stir in the tomato and cook for 2 minutes. Add the Green or Red Chile Sauce, cooked garbanzo beans, and cilantro; reduce heat to low. (See *Ingredients*, page 24, for how to cook garbanzo beans.) Cover; cook the onion and garbanzo mixture for 5 minutes. Salt and pepper the dish according to individual taste. Serve the hot garbanzo beans immediately.

Serves 6

Each serving provides:

88	Calories	16 g	Carbohydrate
5 g	Protein	12 mg	Sodium
1 g	Fat	0 mg	Cholesterol

56

—✥—

Zucchini and Corn Casserole
(Budín de Calabacitas con Elote)

Preparation time: 15 minutes
Cooking time: 10 minutes
Preheat oven to 350°

This brightly colored vegetable dish is quick and easy to prepare and full of savory flavors. A versatile, flavorful vegetable casserole such as this one makes an interesting side dish for an elegant meal or a more informal family dinner. For a healthful, light lunch, serve this appetizing dish with cottage cheese or yogurt. As an interesting variation, add cooked chicken tenderloin pieces, turkey, or shrimp to the casserole for a nutritious, one-dish meal.

1 small white onion, finely chopped
½ cup green onions, finely sliced
1 to 2 cloves garlic, crushed in a garlic press
2 fresh anaheim chiles, seeded, washed, and
    finely chopped
⅛ to 1 fresh serrano or jalapeño chile, seeded,
    washed, and finely chopped (optional, for
    a spicier dish)
1 cup zucchini, halved and finely sliced
1 cup fresh corn kernels
1 cup mushrooms, halved and finely sliced
2 cups Mexican Tomato Sauce (Recipe #17)
1 teaspoon fresh oregano, minced
1 teaspoon fresh thyme, minced

³/₄ cup long-grain rice, cooked
¹/₄ cup lowfat jack cheese, grated
salt and freshly ground pepper

Sauté the white and green onions, garlic, anaheim and
serrano chiles, zucchini, and corn with 2 tablespoons of
water in a large skillet over medium-high heat until the
onions become tender; stir frequently. Stir in the remaining ingredients, excluding the rice and cheese; reduce
heat to low. Salt and pepper the dish according to individual taste.

Spread the cooked rice on the bottom of an ungreased, medium-size casserole dish. Evenly spread the
onion and zucchini mixture over the rice. Sprinkle the
casserole with grated cheese. Bake the casserole uncovered for 10 minutes to melt the cheese. Serve the hot
casserole immediately.

Serves 6

Each serving provides:

114	Calories	20 g	Carbohydrate
6 g	Protein	78 mg	Sodium
2 g	Fat	7 mg	Cholesterol

57

—⚬✿⚬—

Mexican Green Rice

(Arroz Verde)

Preparation time: 10 minutes
Cooking time: 20 minutes

This exotically attractive and elegant dish is a satisfying
version of a rice and chile ambrosia. There are many ways
to serve this dish. As a side dish, this recipe colorfully
complements any meal. For a more festive rice side dish,
you might like to add pink baby shrimp, peas, or broccoli.
For another delicious variation, add pieces of beef, pork,
chicken, or fresh vegetables to invent fun, light, whole-
some meals guaranteed to satisfy the most discriminating
taste buds.

nonstick pan coating
1 small fresh anaheim chile
³/₄ cup long-grain rice, uncooked
1 small white onion, finely chopped
¹/₂ cup green onions, finely sliced
1 to 2 cloves garlic, crushed in a garlic press
¹/₈ to 1 fresh serrano or jalapeño chile, seeded,
      washed, and finely chopped (optional, for
      a spicier dish)
¹/₂ cup Green Chile Sauce (Recipe #15)
1 cup low-salt broth
1 cup water
3 sprigs fresh cilantro, minced (optional)
salt and freshly ground pepper

Preheat the broiler. Evenly spray a large skillet with non-stick pan coating, entirely covering the bottom so ingredients will not stick. Roast the anaheim chile 2 to 3 inches under the broiler for 3 to 4 minutes on each side. Occasionally rotate the chile until it evenly browns and blisters on each side. Put the chile in a tightly closed plastic bag to steam for 5 minutes. Rinse the chile under cold water and carefully peel off the charred skin. Cut off the stem, seed, rinse, and finely chop.

Sauté the rice, white and green onions, garlic, and anaheim and serrano chiles over medium-high heat in the prepared skillet until the rice lightly browns and the onions become tender; stir frequently. Stir in the Green Chile Sauce, broth, and water; mix well. Reduce heat to medium-low. About ½ inch of water should cover the rice. Cover; cook over low heat for 20 minutes until the rice becomes tender and thoroughly absorbs the liquid. Do not let the rice cook dry. If necessary, add additional hot water, ¼ cup at a time, to avoid burning. Salt and pepper the dish according to individual taste. Sprinkle the rice with minced cilantro.

Serves 6

Each serving provides:

66	Calories	15 g	Carbohydrate
2 g	Protein	9 mg	Sodium
0 g	Fat	0 mg	Cholesterol

58

❦

Vermicelli and Vegetables

(Fideo con Verduras)

Preparation time: 20 minutes

Vermicelli noodles, originally introduced by the
Spaniards, were smoothly assimilated into the Mexican
diet. Soaked in the rich, piquant flavors of chiles and
mixed vegetables, vermicelli will delight pasta lovers and
make a welcome addition to enhance any Mexican or
American dish. Serve this as a side dish or increase portions to create a satisfying meal. For extra flavor, serve
your vermicelli dish with a sprinkle of lowfat grated
cheese.

2 ounces vermicelli noodles, uncooked
1 fresh anaheim chile
½ cup celery, finely sliced
1 small bell pepper, quartered, seeded, washed,
    and finely sliced
1 small white onion, finely sliced into rings
1 cup mushrooms, halved and finely sliced
1 to 2 cloves garlic, crushed in a garlic press
½ cup green onions, finely sliced
½ cup Green Chile Sauce (Recipe #15)
1 teaspoon fresh oregano, minced
1 teaspoon fresh thyme, minced
salt and freshly ground pepper

Preheat the broiler. Boil 1½ quarts of water in a large pot.
Add the vermicelli noodles. Cover; cook noodles 7 to 10
minutes until tender; drain well.

Roast the anaheim chile 2 to 3 inches under the broiler for 3 to 4 minutes on each side. Occasionally rotate the chile until it evenly browns and blisters on each side. Put the chile in a tightly closed plastic bag to steam for 5 minutes. Rinse the chile under cold water and carefully peel off the charred skin. Cut off the stem, seed, rinse, and finely chop; set aside.

Place a steamer basket inside a 5-quart pot. Bring 1 inch of water in the pot to the boiling point. Reduce heat to low. Set the celery and bell pepper into the pot on the steamer basket. Cook, partially covered, about 5 minutes. Add the white onions and mushrooms; cook for 3 to 5 minutes until the vegetables are just tender; drain.

Place the garlic and green onions in a large skillet over medium heat. Stir in the anaheim chile, Green Chile Sauce, steamed vegetables, oregano, thyme, and hot vermicelli noodles; combine well. Salt and pepper the dish according to individual taste. Serve the hot vermicelli dish immediately.

Serves 4

Each serving provides:

86	Calories	18 g	Carbohydrate
3 g	Protein	26 mg	Sodium
1 g	Fat	0 mg	Cholesterol

59

❧

Spicy Rice and Beans

(Arroz con Frijoles)

Preparation time: 20 minutes

Rice and beans are a popular, healthful combination found in ancient cuisines in many different countries. This particularly nutritious, appetizing dish probably originates from Caribbean and Mediterranean influences. The chiles and tomatoes enhance this homespun dish to spicy, colorful perfection. This recipe is a meal in itself and a good way to use leftover cooked beans and rice. For an interesting variation, try this special dish with a small portion of marinated chicken strips that have been broiled or grilled over hot coals.

1 large white onion, finely sliced into rings
$^{1}/_{2}$ cup green onions, finely sliced
1 to 2 cloves garlic, minced
2 fresh anaheim chiles, seeded, washed, and
    finely chopped
$^{1}/_{8}$ to 1 fresh serrano or jalapeño chile, seeded,
    washed, and finely chopped (optional, for
    a spicier dish)
2 small ripe tomatoes, blanched or roasted, peeled,
    and finely chopped
$1^{1}/_{2}$ cups Mexican Tomato Sauce (Recipe #17)
$^{1}/_{3}$ cup dried red or pinto beans, cooked
$1^{1}/_{2}$ cups long-grain rice, cooked
1 teaspoon fresh oregano, minced
1 teaspoon fresh thyme, minced

2 to 4 sprigs fresh cilantro
salt and freshly ground pepper

Sauté the white and green onions, garlic, and anaheim
and serrano chiles with 2 tablespoons of water in a large
skillet over medium-high heat until the white onions
become tender; stir frequently. Stir in the remaining
ingredients except cilantro; reduce heat to low. Cook for 5
minutes. Salt and pepper the dish according to individual
taste. Serve the beans and rice dish immediately garnished with fresh cilantro sprigs.

Serves 6

Each serving provides:

98	Calories	26 g	Carbohydrate
3 g	Protein	22 mg	Sodium
0 g	Fat	0 mg	Cholesterol

60

❦

Southwestern Vegetable Medley
(Verduras a la Americana)

Preparation time: 25 minutes

The succulent flavors of these colorful, steamed vegetables are perfect for a one-dish meal served over a warm, soft bed of Mexican or Green Rice. Vegetable lovers will enjoy this awesome feast of steamed vegetables and chiles. For variation, try other fresh vegetables in season. You can also serve this delightful dish with a bowl of fresh salsa.

2 fresh anaheim chiles
2 small red onions, quartered and separated
    into sections
1/2 cup cauliflower, separated into flowerets
1/2 cup broccoli, separated into flowerets
1/2 cup carrots, sliced
1/2 cup celery, julienned
1/2 cup bell peppers, quartered, seeded, washed,
    and cut into strips
1 cup fresh mushroom caps, sliced in half
1/8 to 1 fresh serrano or jalapeño chile, seeded,
    washed, and finely chopped (optional, for
    a spicier dish)
1/4 cup green onions, finely sliced
1 teaspoon fresh thyme, minced
salt and freshly ground pepper

Preheat the broiler. Roast the anaheim chiles 2 to 3 inches under the broiler for 3 to 4 minutes on each side. Occasionally rotate the chiles until they brown and blister on each side. Put the chiles in a tightly closed plastic bag to steam for 5 minutes. Rinse the chiles under cold water and carefully peel off the charred skin. Cut off the stem, seed, rinse, and finely chop; set aside.

Place a steamer basket inside a 5-quart pot. Bring 1 inch of water in the pot to the boiling point; reduce heat to low. Set the onions, cauliflower, broccoli, carrots, celery, and bell peppers on the steamer basket in the pot. Cook the vegetables, partially covered, about 9 minutes. Add mushrooms and cook for 6 to 7 minutes until just tender; drain. Serve the warm vegetables immediately on a platter. Sprinkle the remaining ingredients on top of the steamed vegetables.

Serves 6

Each serving provides:

52	Calories	13 g	Carbohydrate
3 g	Protein	41 mg	Sodium
1 g	Fat	0 mg	Cholesterol

61

—❧—

Roasted Chile Strips
(Rajas de Chile Poblano)

Preparation time: 15 minutes

This is a chile dish in its simplest form. The thin strips of chiles, called *rajas*, are appealing as a side dish packed with vitamin C and complement any meal. If you like, try this exotic dish with strips of grilled chicken served over rice or noodles.

4 large fresh poblano or anaheim chiles
1/8 to 1 fresh serrano or jalapeño chile, seeded, washed, and finely sliced (optional, for a spicier dish)
1 medium white onion, finely sliced into rings
1/2 cup green onions, finely sliced
1 to 2 cloves garlic, crushed in a garlic press
1 medium ripe tomato, blanched or roasted, peeled, and finely chopped
1 teaspoon fresh oregano, minced
1 teaspoon fresh basil, minced
2 sprigs fresh cilantro, minced
salt and freshly ground pepper

Preheat the broiler. Roast the poblano or anaheim chiles 2 to 3 inches under the broiler for 3 to 4 minutes on each side. Occasionally rotate the chiles until they evenly brown and blister on each side. Put the chiles in a tightly closed plastic bag to steam for 5 minutes. Carefully peel off the charred skin. Cut off the stem, seed, rinse, and cut each chile into strips about 1/2 inch wide.

Sauté the serrano chile, white and green onions, and garlic with 2 tablespoons of water in a large skillet over medium-high heat until the white onions are tender. Mix in the remaining ingredients, excluding the cilantro. Salt and pepper according to individual taste. Cover; cook over low heat for 2 minutes. Stir in fresh minced cilantro. Serve the hot dish immediately.

Serves 6

Each serving provides:

33	Calories	5 g	Carbohydrate
1 g	Protein	22 mg	Sodium
0 g	Fat	0 mg	Cholesterol

62

—❧—

Corn and Zucchini Medley

(Revoltillo de Elote con Calabacitas)

Preparation time: 20 minutes

The savory combination of corn, zucchini, and chiles served as a side dish nicely complements many nutritious Mexican dishes. For another tasty variation, sprinkle low-fat, grated jack cheese over the cooked vegetables. Serve this dish alone or over noodles or rice. For a fully satisfying meal, serve this dish with a poultry, seafood, or beef main dish and a garden-fresh salad.

2 cups zucchini, finely sliced
1 cup fresh corn, uncooked
1 small white onion, finely sliced into rings
½ cup green onions, finely sliced
1 fresh anaheim chile, seeded, washed, and sliced
1 cup mushrooms, finely sliced
⅛ to 1 fresh serrano or jalapeño chile, seeded,
    washed, and finely sliced (optional, for a
    spicier dish)
1 to 2 cloves garlic, crushed in a garlic press
2 medium ripe tomatoes, finely chopped
1 teaspoon fresh oregano, minced
1 teaspoon fresh thyme, minced
salt and freshly ground pepper

Place a steamer basket inside a 5-quart pot. Bring 1 inch of water in the pot to the boiling point. Reduce heat to low. Place the zucchini and corn into the pot on the steamer basket. Cook the vegetables, partially covered, for 4 minutes. Add the white and green onions, anaheim chile, and mushrooms; cook the vegetables 3 to 4 minutes until just tender. Place the vegetables on a large platter.

Sauté the serrano chile, garlic, tomatoes, oregano, and thyme in a small saucepan over medium-high heat for 2 minutes; stir frequently. Salt and pepper the dish according to individual taste. Serve the hot tomato sauce over the steamed vegetables immediately.

Serves 6

Each serving provides:

59	Calories	14 g	Carbohydrate
3 g	Protein	17 mg	Sodium
1 g	Fat	0 mg	Cholesterol

63

⎯⎯ ❦ ⎯⎯

Pinto Beans

(Frijoles)

Preparation time: 10 minutes
Soaking time: Overnight
Cooking time: 2 1/2 to 3 hours

The humble pinto bean retains its mighty position as an integral part of most Mexican meals. Beans provide one of the richest sources of vegetable protein, ounce for ounce. Paired with rice or corn you have an unbeatable, healthful combination. You can serve these easy-to-prepare, flavorful beans on tostadas, stuffed in burritos and tacos, or alone to complement any appetizing Mexican meal. It is easy to enjoy these simple, nutritious, tasty beans.

1 cup dry pinto beans, uncooked
water
salt and freshly ground pepper

Pick through the beans to remove rocks and cracked or hard beans. Wash the beans and place them in a 3-quart pot with enough water to cover the beans; soak overnight. Drain the water and rinse beans again. Place the beans in a medium-size saucepan; add enough fresh water to cover the beans by about 2 inches. Remove any beans or pieces that float to the top. Cover; bring beans to a boil and cook 3 minutes; reduce heat to medium-low. Simmer gently about 2 1/2 to 3 hours; stir frequently. Add more boiling water if the water cooks away.

When beans are soft enough to smash easily between the thumb and index finger when pressed with slight pressure, remove from heat. There should be only enough water to cover just 2 to 3 inches below the surface of the beans. The amount of liquid remaining in the pot will determine how soupy the beans become. Mash the beans with a potato masher until the mixture becomes a smooth, soupy paste. Salt and pepper the beans according to individual taste. Serve the hot beans immediately.

Serves 6

Each ½-cup serving provides:

98	Calories	19 g	Carbohydrate
6 g	Protein	7 mg	Sodium
0 g	Fat	0 mg	Cholesterol

64

✦

Spicy Pinto Beans
(Frijoles Picante)

Preparation time: 10 minutes
Soaking time: Overnight
Cooking time: 2¹/₂ to 3 hours

Take a simple, tasty plate of beans and make it even more savory and sensational with the rich flavor of a piquant Mexican Tomato Sauce. Easy to prepare, this recipe will satisfy the most discriminating pinto bean lover.

1 cup dry pinto beans
water
¹/₂ cup Mexican Tomato Sauce (Recipe #17)
salt and freshly ground pepper

Pick through the beans to remove rocks and cracked or hard beans. Wash the beans and place them in a 3-quart pot with enough water to cover the beans; soak overnight. Drain the water and rinse the beans again. Place the beans in a medium-size saucepan; add enough fresh water to cover the beans by about 2 inches. Remove any beans or pieces that float to the top. Cover; bring beans to a boil and cook 3 minutes; reduce heat to medium-low. Simmer the beans gently for 2¹/₂ to 3 hours; stir frequently. Add more boiling water if the water cooks away.

    Warm the Mexican Tomato Sauce in a small saucepan. When the beans are soft enough to smash easily between the thumb and index finger when pressed with slight pressure, remove from heat; drain. Stir in the Mexican Tomato Sauce. Salt and pepper the beans according to individual taste. Serve the hot beans immediately.

Serves 6

Each serving provides:

103	Calories	19 g	Carbohydrate
6 g	Protein	7 mg	Sodium
0 g	Fat	0 mg	Cholesterol

65

—❧—

Stuffed Chiles Casserole
(Budín de Chiles Rellenos)

Preparation time: 15 minutes
Cooking time: 20 minutes
Preheat oven to 350°

Different from the more typical stuffed chiles combination, this casserole dish offers a versatile, appealing, easy-
to-prepare meal, with fewer calories and less fat than the
better known Chile Rellenos dish. The contrasting textures and flavors of this light and puffy casserole are
delightful. Wait until you bite into a chile followed by the
lingering taste of melted cheese. Every bite is sinfully
delicious. Cut the casserole into squares and serve the
squares with a bowl of fresh salsa. A fresh dinner salad
and beans nicely complement this meal. For another
attractive variation, serve the Stuffed Chiles Casserole
squares over Mexican Rice (#52).

nonstick pan coating
4 fresh anaheim chiles
1 medium white onion, finely chopped
½ cup green onions, finely sliced
1 to 2 cloves garlic, crushed in a garlic press
⅛ to 1 fresh serrano or jalapeño chile, seeded,
        washed, and finely chopped (optional, for a
        spicier dish)
½ pound (8 ounces) lowfat Jack cheese
2 medium eggs, separated
salt and freshly ground pepper

Preheat the broiler. Evenly spray a 1½-quart square, glass baking dish with nonstick pan coating, entirely covering the bottom so eggs will not stick. Roast the anaheim chiles 2 to 3 inches under the broiler for 3 to 4 minutes on each side. Occasionally rotate the chiles until they evenly brown and blister on each side. Put the chiles in a tightly closed plastic bag to steam for 5 minutes. Carefully peel off the charred skin. Cut off the stem, seed, rinse, and cut each chile into four strips; set aside.

Sauté the white and green onions, garlic, and serrano chiles with 1 tablespoon of water in a large skillet over medium-high heat until the white onions become tender; remove the onion mixture from the heat. Spoon the sautéed onion mixture evenly into the prepared baking dish. Cut half the cheese into sixteen cubes. Wrap each strip of chile around a cube of cheese and lay them atop the onions. Beat the egg whites until stiff. Beat egg yolks slightly and fold them into the stiffly beaten whites. Spoon the egg mixture evenly over the chiles. Grate the remaining cheese and sprinkle it over the casserole. Salt and pepper the dish according to individual taste. Bake casserole in preheated oven for 20 minutes. Cut the casserole into squares.

Serves 6

Each serving provides:

157	Calories	7 g	Carbohydrate
14 g	Protein	267 mg	Sodium
8 g	Fat	90 mg	Cholesterol

66

❦

Stuffed Zucchini
(Calabacitas Rellenas)

Preparation time: 15 minutes
Cooking time: 20 minutes
Preheat oven to 350°

The chiles, cilantro, and tomatoes in this attractive dish give the simple zucchini extra zest and flavor. Serve the stuffed zucchini as a side dish to complement your next Mexican dinner. For extra flavor, sprinkle with lowfat grated cheese.

3 medium zucchinis
1 medium white onion, finely sliced into rings
$^1/_2$ cup green onions, finely sliced
1 to 2 cloves garlic, crushed in a garlic press
1 fresh anaheim chile, seeded, washed, and
    finely sliced
$^1/_8$ to 1 fresh serrano or jalapeño chile, seeded,
    washed, and finely sliced (optional, for a
    spicier dish)
$^1/_2$ cup Mexican Tomato Sauce (Recipe #17)
2 sprigs fresh cilantro, minced (optional)
1 medium ripe tomato, blanched or roasted, peeled,
    and finely chopped
1 teaspoon fresh oregano, minced
1 teaspoon fresh thyme, minced
salt and freshly ground pepper

Clean zucchini in cold water, cut in half lengthwise, and carefully scoop out the middle with a spoon; dice the zucchini pulp. Sauté the zucchini pulp, white and green onions, garlic, and anaheim and serrano chiles with 2 tablespoons of water over medium-high heat in a large skillet until the onions become tender; stir frequently. Mix in remaining ingredients. Salt and pepper the dish according to individual taste.

Stuff the zucchini with equal portions of the sautéed cooked onion and tomato mixture. Place the stuffed zucchinis in a large, ungreased casserole dish. Bake in preheated oven for 20 minutes until tender. Serve the hot dish immediately.

Serves 6

Each serving provides:

37	Calories	8 g	Carbohydrate
2 g	Protein	13 mg	Sodium
0 g	Fat	0 mg	Cholesterol

67

❦

Mexican-style Potatoes
(Papas con Chiles)

Preparation time: 15 minutes
Cooking time: 30 minutes

Mexican Potatoes, though not as well known as other traditional Mexican dishes, are found on many Mexican
street corners on outdoor grills with Mexican sausages
(chorizo), chiles, or onions. Here is an easy way to prepare
a healthful, scrumptious side dish of potatoes with chiles.
This recipe will embellish any meal to perfection. If you
like, use the leftover potatoes in an omelet, scrambled
eggs, soup, or stew.

3 medium potatoes, washed and unskinned
3 fresh anaheim chiles
1 small white onion, finely chopped
$^1/_2$ cup green onions, finely sliced
1 clove garlic, crushed in a garlic press
$^1/_4$ to 2 fresh serrano or jalapeño chiles, seeded,
        washed, and finely chopped
2 to 4 sprigs fresh cilantro, minced (optional)
salt and freshly ground pepper

Preheat the broiler. Wash the potatoes. Boil enough water
in a large saucepan to cover the potatoes by 2 to 3 inches;
reduce heat to medium. Cook potatoes with skins for 30
minutes until tender; drain well. Wash, peel, and dice
potatoes into $1^1/_2$-inch pieces.
  Roast anaheim chiles 2 to 3 inches under the broiler
for 3 to 4 minutes on each side. Occasionally rotate the

chiles until they evenly brown and blister on each side. Put the chiles in a tightly closed plastic bag to steam for 5 minutes. Carefully peel off the charred skin. Cut off the stems, seed, rinse, and finely chop.

Sauté the white and green onions, garlic, and anaheim and serrano chiles with 2 tablespoons of water in a medium-size skillet over medium-high heat until the onions become tender; stir frequently. Stir in the warm potatoes and cilantro; reduce heat to low. Cook potato mixture for 2 minutes; stir occasionally. Salt and pepper the dish according to individual taste. Serve the hot potatoes immediately.

Serves 6

Each serving provides:

78	Calories	18 g	Carbohydrate
2 g	Protein	28 mg	Sodium
0 g	Fat	0 mg	Cholesterol

68

❧

Spicy Green Beans
and Mushrooms

(Ejotes con Hongos)

Preparation time: 20 minutes

Lemon juice really perks up this popular combination of
green beans and mushrooms. Buy fresh, young green
beans without blemishes. Leftovers of this recipe are a
great addition to a stew, soup, or salad.

1½ pounds green beans, cleaned and cut
    diagonally into 2-inch pieces
1 small white onion, finely sliced
¼ cup green onions, finely sliced
1 clove garlic, crushed in a garlic press
1 cup mushrooms, finely sliced
⅛ to 1 fresh serrano or jalapeño chile, seeded,
    washed, and finely chopped (optional, for
    a spicier dish)
2 tablespoons lemon juice
salt and freshly ground pepper

Place a steamer basket inside a 5-quart pot. Bring 1 inch
of water in the pot to the boiling point; reduce heat to
low. Place the green beans on the steamer basket. Cover;
steam 5 minutes. Add remaining ingredients, excluding

the lemon juice. Cook the green beans for 5 to 7 minutes until just tender, not soft. Lift the vegetables out of the steamer and serve the hot dish immediately. Sprinkle each serving with lemon juice.

Serves 6

Each serving provides:

45	Calories	10 g	Carbohydrate
2 g	Protein	25 mg	Sodium
0 g	Fat	0 mg	Cholesterol

Mexican Meat Dishes

The Spaniards were the first to introduce domesticated animals, such as pigs, lambs, goats, and cattle to the local Indians. Over the centuries, the Indians have exquisitely blended their favorite, healthful ingredients with an assortment of meat. Today, meat remains popular throughout Mexico and is readily available in most of the larger towns and cities. In the smaller towns, meat is not always available or affordable. The local folk continue to largely subsist on a simpler diet of corn, beans, vegetables, and chiles.

Mexicans are avid pork lovers and have several traditional recipes that present the dazzling flavor of succulent pork simmered for hours in a rich-flavored sauce. Other meat combinations are equally coveted dishes that will make special culinary events even more festive, colorful, and flavorful. Food stands appear on virtually every large city street corner in Mexico. They offer a selection of slowly simmered meats soaked in spicy, tantalizing sauces. In the north, the beef is tender, packed with extra flavor, and often grilled as steaks. In the south, the beef is stringier and often used for taco, burrito, or taquito fillings and other favorite Mexican dishes.

However tasty, meats are high in saturated fat and known to cause high levels of cholesterol, high blood pressure, and heart disease. Proper selection and preparation of meat is important for controlling the amounts of saturated fat and cholesterol in one's daily diet. Health-conscious cooks should use smaller portions of extra-lean meats without visible fat and marbling. Even without the fat, you will discover that meat dishes can still be deliciously succulent after soaking in savory chile sauces.

The recipes found in *Mexican Meat Dishes* present a sample of easy-to-prepare, spicy, appetizing meat dishes. Most of these recipes are low-calorie versions of traditional fare. The lowfat recipes in this section reduce portions of meat and do not use lard or oils to fry or roast meats. These recipes show cooks how to broil, grill, sauté, or cook meats with spicy chile sauces. Use these fascinating recipes to introduce your family and friends to your exquisite mastery of Mexican cuisine.

Mexican Meat Dishes

69

— ❧ —

Pork in Green Chile Sauce

(Carnitas en Salsa Verde)

Preparation time: 10 minutes
Cooking time: 35 minutes
Preheat oven to 375°

This recipe is a "light" version of a very popular, classical Mexican dish. The chunks of pork, heavily soaked in a savory Green Chile Sauce, will satisfy your desire for the blended flavors of spicy chiles and pork. Quick and easy to prepare, this colorful and tempting pork dish is particularly memorable when eaten with a warmed corn or flour tortilla, Mexican Rice (#52), and a small salad. Consider substituting the Green Chile Sauce with Red Chile Sauce (#16) for another popular, savory variation of this special Mexican dish. For variety, you can use chicken or turkey instead of pork.

3 cups Green Chile Sauce (Recipe #15)
1 medium white onion, halved and finely sliced
1/2 cup green onions, finely sliced
1 to 2 cloves garlic, crushed in a garlic press
1 pound lean loin of pork, cut into 1 1/2-inch cubes
1 teaspoon fresh oregano, minced
salt and freshly ground pepper

Combine all the ingredients in an ungreased casserole dish with a cover. Salt and pepper the dish according to taste. Cover; bake the pork dish in preheated oven for

35 minutes, until the pork cooks thoroughly and becomes tender; stir occasionally. Serve the hot pork dish immediately.

Serves 6

Each serving provides:

174   Calories   8 g   Carbohydrate
23 g Protein   68 mg Sodium
4 g   Fat   60 mg Cholesterol

70

※

Mexican Meat Loaf
(Albondigón)

Preparation time: 10 minutes
Baking time: 1 hour
Preheat oven to 350°

Home-cooked meat loaf is an inviting dinner in any country. The chiles and Mexican Tomato Sauce add extra zip to this time-honored American family dinner. Use thinly sliced leftovers to create a mouth-watering sandwich for your next lunch or a quick late-night snack.

$\frac{1}{2}$ cup Mexican Tomato Sauce (Recipe #17)
1 medium egg
$\frac{1}{3}$ cup dry bread crumbs or crackers
1 to 2 cloves garlic, minced
$\frac{1}{8}$ to 1 fresh serrano or jalapeño chile, seeded, washed, and finely chopped (optional, for a spicier dish)
1 teaspoon fresh oregano, minced
2 sprigs fresh cilantro, minced (optional)
$1\frac{1}{2}$ pounds extra-lean ground round
1 small white onion, finely chopped
$\frac{1}{4}$ cup green onions, finely sliced
salt and freshly ground pepper

Thoroughly combine all the ingredients, excluding $\frac{1}{4}$ cup of the green onions and $\frac{1}{4}$ cup of the Mexican Tomato Sauce, in a medium-size bowl. Salt and pepper the dish according to individual taste. Pack the meat mixture down firmly in an 8- by 4- by 3-inch loaf pan. Use a spoon to evenly spread the remaining Mexican Tomato Sauce over the top of the meat loaf. Bake the meat loaf in preheated oven for 1 hour. Drain any excess fat from the loaf pan. Let the meat loaf stand 5 minutes before serving. Garnish each serving of meat loaf with the remaining green onions.

Serves 6

Each serving provides:

227	Calories	5 g	Carbohydrate
35 g	Protein	119 mg	Sodium
6 g	Fat	110 mg	Cholesterol

71

❦

Jalapeño Hamburgers
(Hamburguesas con Jalapeños)

Preparation time: 10 minutes
Cooking time: 10 to 15 minutes

Jalapeño chiles give this popular all-American recipe an
exotic new flair. Liven up your dull hamburger and
impress your friends with this terrific recipe. The ham-
burgers look festive because the chiles add color and contrast to the hamburger meat. If you find jalapeño chiles
too spicy, you can use anaheim chiles as a milder substitute. For another fun variation, try adding finely chopped
mushrooms.

¹/₄ cup Mexican Tomato Sauce (Recipe #17)
1 small white onion, minced
¹/₈ cup green onions, finely sliced
1 to 2 cloves garlic, minced
¹/₄ to ¹/₂ fresh jalapeño chile, seeded, washed,
     and finely chopped
2 to 4 sprigs fresh cilantro, minced (optional)
1¹/₂ pounds extra-lean ground round
salt and freshly ground pepper

Thoroughly combine all the ingredients in a medium-size
bowl. Salt and pepper the dish according to individual
taste. Pat the meat mixture into six hamburger patties.
Preheat a large, ungreased skillet over medium-high heat
until just hot. Heat to the point that the meat will sizzle
when you put it into the skillet. Place the meat patties in
the skillet and brown on each side for 3 to 4 minutes;

reduce heat to medium. Continue cooking meat on both sides for 2 to 3 minutes until cooked thoroughly according to individual taste.

Serves 6

Each serving provides:

205	Calories	3 g	Carbohydrate
34 g	Protein	79 mg	Sodium
5 g	Fat	80 mg	Cholesterol

72

Red Stew
(Mole Rojo)

Preparation time: 20 minutes
Cooking time: 10 to 15 minutes

Mole is not just a well-known chocolate sauce served by everyone from Montezuma to Hernán Cortés. It's much more than that. Mole is a sauce made with chiles that when heated slowly combines the rich flavors of the colorful ingredients. This satisfying meal is a family recipe and suggests the Mexican love of pork. Try substituting beef or turkey for an appetizing variation.

1 fresh anaheim chile
½ pound extra-lean pork, cubed
1 to 2 cloves garlic, crushed in a garlic press
4 medium ripe tomatoes, blanched or roasted,
     peeled, and chopped
1 medium white onion, chopped
½ cup green onions, finely sliced
⅛ to 1 fresh serrano or jalapeño chile, seeded,
     washed, and finely chopped (optional, for
     a spicier dish)
1 teaspoon fresh oregano, minced
½ cup lean chicken, skinned, boned, and cut
     into pieces
1 cup fresh celery, finely sliced
1 cup fresh corn, uncooked
2 to 5 sprigs fresh cilantro
salt and freshly ground pepper

Preheat the broiler. Roast the anaheim chile 2 to 3 inches under the broiler for 3 to 4 minutes on each side. Occasionally rotate the chile until it evenly browns and blisters on each side. Put the chile in a tightly closed plastic bag to steam for 5 minutes. Carefully peel off the charred skin. Cut off the stem, seed, rinse, and coarsely chop; set aside.

Simmer the pork for 30 minutes with enough water to almost cover it. Drain pork while reserving the stock. Combine the garlic, tomatoes, white and green onions, anaheim and serrano chiles, and oregano in a large bowl. Purée half of the vegetable mixture in a blender; set aside. Sauté the chicken, celery, and corn in a large skillet over medium-high heat for 3 minutes; stir frequently. Reduce heat to low. Stir the unpuréed vegetable mixture into the bowl; cook 3 minutes; combine well. Stir in the purée and the reserved pork stock.

Place the pork in the center of the skillet surrounded by the chicken mixture. Cover; cook the stew over low heat for 10 to 15 minutes until the chicken and pork become tender. Salt and pepper according to taste. Serve the stew from a shallow tureen garnished with fresh cilantro sprigs.

Serves 6

Each serving provides:

157	Calories	21 g	Carbohydrate
20 g	Protein	72 mg	Sodium
3 g	Fat	46 mg	Cholesterol

73

❧

Mexican Stew
(Guisado de Mexicana)

Preparation time: 15 minutes
Cooking time: 20 to 25 minutes

Like most stews, this fragrant and colorful dish offers a hearty and filling meal. Packed with slow-simmered flavor, this stew offers a flavorful temptation for a special, informal feast. Add a fresh salad and a full-bodied, red wine to the menu to make this an absolutely perfect meal.

2 fresh anaheim chiles
3/4 pound extra-lean round steak, cut into
    1 1/2-inch cubes
2 medium white onions, chopped
1/2 cup green onions, finely sliced
1 to 2 cloves garlic, crushed in a garlic press
1/8 to 1 fresh serrano or jalapeño chile, seeded,
    washed, and finely chopped (optional, for a
    spicier dish)
2 medium ripe tomatoes, finely chopped
1 cup corn, uncooked
1 1/2 cups green beans, uncooked
1 cup low-salt broth
1 teaspoon fresh oregano, minced
1 sprig fresh cilantro, minced
salt and freshly ground pepper

Preheat the broiler. Roast the anaheim chiles 2 to 3 inches under the broiler for 3 to 4 minutes on each side. Occasionally rotate each chile until they evenly brown and blister on each side. Put the chiles in a tightly closed plastic bag to steam for 5 minutes. Carefully peel off the charred skin. Cut off the stem, seed, rinse, and cut the chiles into 2-inch strips; set aside.

Heat a large skillet over medium-high heat. Evenly brown the meat to sear in the juices; turn frequently. Add the white and green onions, garlic, and anaheim and serrano chiles. Sauté the meat and onion mixture until the onions become tender; stir frequently. Stir in the tomatoes; cook 2 minutes. Mix in remaining ingredients; reduce heat to low. Cover; simmer meat mixture for 20 to 25 minutes, stirring occasionally, until the meat is tender. Salt and pepper the dish according to individual taste.

Serves 6

Each serving provides:

179	Calories	17 g	Carbohydrate
20 g	Protein	56 mg	Sodium
3 g	Fat	39 mg	Cholesterol

74

❧

Meat with Chile

(Carne con Chile)

Preparation time: 20 minutes
Cooking time: 30 to 45 minutes

Popularly known in America as Chile con Carne, this
simple, flavorful dish is a mellow blend of meat, tomatoes,
chiles, garlic, and onions. What a sumptuous treat! If you
like, you can substitute the pinto beans with red, white, or
kidney beans and the beef with pork or chicken. Serve
this nourishing, time-honored dish with a garden-fresh
salad, chunk of french bread, and fruit.

½ pound extra-lean ground round
1 medium white onion, chopped
½ cup green onions, finely sliced
1 to 3 cloves garlic, crushed in a garlic press
⅛ to 1 fresh serrano or jalapeño chile, seeded,
    washed, and finely chopped (optional, for a
    spicier dish)
3½ cups Mexican Tomato Sauce (Recipe #17)
5 medium ripe tomatoes, blanched or roasted,
    peeled, and quartered
1 cup pinto beans, cooked
1 teaspoon cumin (optional)
1 teaspoon fresh oregano, minced
2 to 4 sprigs fresh cilantro, minced (optional)
salt and freshly ground pepper

Heat a 5-quart cooking pot over medium-high heat.
Stirring frequently, evenly brown the meat to sear in the

juices; drain off the excess fat. Add the white and green onions, garlic, and serrano chile. Mix in the remaining ingredients. Salt and pepper the dish according to individual taste. Cover; simmer the chile dish gently for 30 to 45 minutes, stirring occasionally.

Serves 7

Each serving provides:

177	Calories	20 g	Carbohydrate
19 g	Protein	57 mg	Sodium
3 g	Fat	34 mg	Cholesterol

75

—✧—

Beef Stew with Chiles
(Guisado de Carne con Chiles)

Preparation time: 20 minutes
Cooking time: 30 minutes

This is a simple version of a hearty and savory beef stew.
The blended flavors of the Mexican Tomato Sauce and
chiles enhance the beef stew to satisfying perfection. For
variety you can replace the beef with extra-lean pork,
chicken, or ham. To complete your meal, serve the stew
with a crisp salad and rice or beans. This recipe is also
great served over cooked pasta.

³/₄ pound extra-lean round steak, cut into
    1¹/₂-inch cubes
1 medium white onion, finely sliced
¹/₂ cup green onions, finely sliced
1 to 2 cloves garlic, crushed in a garlic press
2 fresh anaheim chiles, seeded, washed, and chopped
¹/₈ to 1 fresh serrano or jalapeño chile, seeded,
    washed, and finely chopped (optional, for a
    spicier dish)
1 cup celery, sliced
1 cup fresh mushrooms, sliced
1 medium ripe tomato, blanched or roasted, peeled,
    and chopped
1 cup corn
1 cup Mexican Tomato Sauce (Recipe #17)
¹/₂ cup Red Chile Sauce (Recipe #16)
1 cup water
1 teaspoon fresh oregano, minced

1 teaspoon fresh basil, minced
salt and freshly ground pepper

Heat a 5- to 6-quart cooking pot over medium-high heat.
Evenly brown the meat to sear in the juices; turn frequently. Add the white and green onions, garlic, anaheim
and serrano chiles, celery, and mushrooms. Sauté the
mixture until the onions become tender; stir frequently.
Stir in the tomato; cook 2 minutes. Mix in the remaining
ingredients; reduce heat to low. Cover; simmer the stew
for 30 minutes; stir occasionally. Salt and pepper the dish
according to individual taste. Serve the hot stew immediately.

Serves 6

Each serving provides:

171	Calories	17 g	Carbohydrate
20 g	Protein	73 mg	Sodium
3 g	Fat	39 mg	Cholesterol

76

—✦—

Beef with Potatoes and Chiles

(Carne con Papas y Chiles)

Preparation time: 20 minutes

Try this satisfying, fragrant, hearty dish. Hot and steaming, this stew is perfect for an old-fashioned family dinner served in a large soup tureen. You might like to substitute the beef with pork, chicken, or turkey for an appetizing variation. Add a fresh salad and a full-bodied red wine to the menu to create a perfect meal.

¾ pound extra-lean round steak, cut into
    ½-inch strips
1 cup carrots, sliced
2 medium cooked potatoes, chopped into
    1-inch pieces
1 medium white onion, chopped
½ cup green onions, finely sliced
1 to 2 cloves garlic, crushed in a garlic press
⅛ to 1 fresh serrano or jalapeño chile, seeded,
    washed, and finely chopped (optional, for
    a spicier dish)
2 fresh anaheim chiles, seeded, washed, and
    finely chopped
½ cup Red Chile Sauce (Recipe #16)
1 medium ripe tomato, blanched or roasted,
    peeled, and chopped
1 teaspoon fresh oregano, minced
1 teaspoon fresh thyme, minced
salt and freshly ground pepper

Heat a large skillet over medium-high heat. Evenly brown the meat to sear in the juices; turn frequently. Add the carrots and potatoes; stir frequently for 3 minutes. Add the white and green onions, garlic, and serrano and anaheim chiles. Sauté the mixture until the onions become tender; reduce heat to low. Mix in remaining ingredients and cook for 2 to 5 minutes until the carrots are just tender. Salt and pepper to taste. Serve the dish hot.

Serves 6

Each serving provides:			
172	Calories	18 g	Carbohydrate
19 g	Protein	57 mg	Sodium
3 g	Fat	39 mg	Cholesterol

77

— ❧ —

Beef in Red Chile Sauce

(Carnitas en Salsa de Chile Rojo)

Preparation time: 15 minutes
Cooking time: 20 to 25 minutes

This recipe is a slimmed-down version of a very popular
and traditional Mexican dish. You will find that the
chunks of meat, heavily soaked in rich Red Chile Sauce,
offer a tantalizing sensation with every mouth-watering
bite. Quick and easy to prepare, this colorful, tempting
beef and Red Chile Sauce dish tastes especially marvelous
when eaten with a warmed corn or flour tortilla. For side
dishes, try Mexican Green Rice (#57) and a small salad.
Consider substituting the Red Chile Sauce with Green
Chile Sauce (#15) as an excellent variation of this special,
savory Mexican dish.

1¼ pounds extra-lean round steak, cut into
     1½-inch cubes
1 medium white onion, thinly sliced
½ cup green onions, thinly sliced
1 to 2 cloves garlic, crushed in a garlic press
2½ cups Red Chile Sauce (Recipe #15)
1 teaspoon fresh oregano, minced
salt and freshly ground pepper

Heat a large skillet over medium-high heat. Evenly brown
the meat to sear in the juices; turn frequently. Stir in the
white and green onions and garlic with 2 tablespoons of
water until the white onions become tender; drain off the
excess fat. Stir in the remaining ingredients. Cover; simmer

gently for 20 to 25 minutes, until the beef is tender and pulls apart with a fork. Salt and pepper the dish according to individual taste. Serve the hot beef dish immediately.

Serves 6

Each serving provides:

190	Calories	7 g	Carbohydrate
29 g	Protein	72 mg	Sodium
5 g	Fat	66 mg	Cholesterol

78

—❧—

Mexican-style Meat
(Picadillo)

Preparation time: 25 minutes
Cooking time: 30 to 45 minutes

I like to use this recipe as a savory Mexican-style spaghetti sauce. You can also serve this versatile dish alone, on a salad, or over cooked rice. This sauce stores well in the refrigerator or freezer and is handy for lunch or dinner, especially when you find yourself hungry and in a hurry. Reduce the amount of Mexican Tomato Sauce and tomatoes and this versatile recipe makes a great spicy filling for tacos, tostadas, or burritos.

2 fresh anaheim chiles
5 medium ripe tomatoes, blanched or roasted, peeled
1 to 2 cloves garlic, crushed in a garlic press
1 pound extra-lean ground round
1 medium white onion, chopped
¹/₂ cup green onions, finely sliced
¹/₈ to 1 fresh serrano or jalapeño chile, seeded,
     washed, and finely chopped (optional, for
     a spicier dish)
2 cups Mexican Tomato Sauce (Recipe #17)
1 cup mushrooms, sliced
2 to 5 sprigs fresh cilantro, minced (optional)
1 teaspoon fresh oregano, minced
1 teaspoon fresh thyme, minced
2 bay leaves
salt and freshly ground pepper

Preheat the broiler. Roast the anaheim chiles 2 to 3 inches under the broiler for 3 to 4 minutes on each side. Occasionally rotate the chiles until they evenly brown and blister on each side. Put the chiles in a tightly closed plastic bag to steam for 5 minutes. Carefully peel off the charred skin. Cut off the stems, seed, rinse, and finely chop; set aside.

Purée 2 of the tomatoes and garlic. Heat a large skillet over medium-high heat. Turning frequently, evenly brown the meat to sear in the juices; drain off the excess fat. Add the white and green onions and anaheim and serrano chiles. Sauté the mixture until the onions become tender. Add the remaining tomatoes, chopped; cook for 2 minutes. Stir in the tomato purée and remaining ingredients; reduce heat to low. Cover; simmer the meat sauce gently for 30 to 45 minutes, stirring occasionally; remove the bay leaves. Salt and pepper the dish according to individual taste. Serve the hot meat sauce immediately.

Serves 7

Each serving provides:

166	Calories	13 g	Carbohydrate
21 g	Protein	63 mg	Sodium
4 g	Fat	45 mg	Cholesterol

79

—✢—

Spicy Mexican-style Steak
(Carne Asada)

Preparation time: 15 minutes
Refrigeration time: 30 minutes
Grilling time: 10 to 12 minutes

Broiled or grilled dishes are becoming increasingly attractive because they are tasty and lower in fat and calories. A tangy marinade of lime juice perks up the flavor of the extra-lean meat. Serve these tangy, grilled steaks with a crisp salad, beans, or rice. For an elegant dinner, serve the grilled meat pieces with a cushion of fluffy, cooked rice and a fresh, colorful salsa. If you cannot grill outdoors, you can broil the steaks 4 to 5 inches under the broiler or in a cast-iron grill pan.

$1/3$ cup lime juice
6 small, thin, extra-lean round or flank steaks
    ($1^1/2$ pounds)
8 sprigs fresh cilantro, minced (optional)
1 medium white onion, halved and thinly sliced
$1/2$ cup green onions, finely sliced
1 to 2 cloves garlic, crushed in a garlic press
$1/8$ to 1 fresh serrano or jalapeño chile, seeded, washed,
    and finely chopped (optional, for a spicier dish)
1 fresh anaheim chile, seeded, washed, and
    finely chopped
$1/3$ cup Green Chile Sauce (Recipe #15)
1 medium tomato, blanched or roasted, seeded,
    and finely chopped
salt and freshly ground pepper

Place the lime juice and steaks in a rectangular, glass baking dish. Rub the steaks in the marinade to coat the steaks with the juices. Cover and marinate the steaks in the refrigerator for 30 minutes; turn the steaks occasionally.

Mince 2 sprigs of cilantro. Sauté the remaining ingredients, excluding the Green Chile Sauce, tomato, and cilantro, with 2 tablespoons of water in a saucepan over medium-high heat until the white onions become tender; stir frequently. Add the Green Chile Sauce, tomato, and the 2 sprigs of minced cilantro. Continue to cook the Green Chile Sauce and onion mixture for 2 minutes; reduce heat to low. Salt and pepper the sauce mixture according to individual taste.

Remove the steaks from the marinade; drain. Place the steaks 4 or 5 inches from a bed of hot coals. Sear both sides of each steak for 1 minute. Continue to grill the steaks for 4 to 5 minutes on each side until the meat cooks thoroughly according to individual taste. Place the grilled steaks on six oven-warmed plates. Attractively smother the steaks with the hot Green Chile Sauce and onion mixture. Garnish the steaks with the remaining fresh cilantro sprigs.

Serves 6

Each serving provides:

220	Calories	7 g	Carbohydrate
34 g	Protein	80 mg	Sodium
6 g	Fat	79 mg	Cholesterol

Mexican Poultry Dishes

Wild game birds like small turkeys, quail, partridges, and ducks are indigenous to Mexico. In the sixteenth century, the Spanish conqueror of Mexico enthusiastically described the abundance of fowl upon his arrival in the new land. The Spaniards watched the native Indians prepare tasty, exotic poultry dishes smothered in spicy chiles and tomatoes. Turkey, soaked in a savory mole sauce, was a royal delicacy prepared especially for the Aztec nobility in the palace at Tenochtitlán.

The Spaniards were the first to introduce the domesticated chicken to the local Indians. The Indians, already avid poultry lovers, easily assimilated this bird into their excellent diet. Today, poultry remains popular throughout Mexico. Like many Americans, Mexican cooks often prepare turkey to celebrate special holidays. Versatile, affordable, and quick-cooking, chicken is increasingly popular and an undisputed American and Mexican favorite.

Poultry is lower than pork and beef in saturated fat and cholesterol. Chicken and turkey are an especially important, lean source of complete protein, vitamins, and minerals. Always remove the skin from poultry before cooking to significantly reduce the quantity of saturated fat and cholesterol present. Without the skin, 64 percent of the calories from chicken are from protein and 31 percent of the calories are from fat. Skinned and deboned, the white meat is leaner with lower amounts of fat and cholesterol than the dark meat. Pieces of breast are the leanest cuts of chicken. Avoid eating chicken organ parts, like hearts, liver, and kidneys, because they contain concentrated amounts of cholesterol.

The recipes offered in *Mexican Poultry Dishes* present a variety of easy-to-prepare, spicy dishes using poultry. Most of the recipes are for chicken; however, you can easily substitute turkey or other poultry. The different cuisines around the world present many thousands of ways to use poultry. In Mexico, poultry specialities are numerous and especially appealing when uniquely combined with chiles and a common variety of fresh vegetables, fruits, grains, and dairy products. However, it is the spicy chiles that add a distinctive, desirable zest to the milder flavor of poultry. This section presents ideas on how to prepare tantalizing low-calorie, lowfat poultry dishes. Here is your chance to create mouth-watering, nutritious meals or to discover new appetizing ways to prepare great poultry dishes.

Mexican Poultry Dishes

80

—❦—

Spicy Turkey Vermicelli
(Fideo con Pavo)

Preparation time: 15 minutes

Turkey and vermicelli noodles are a perfect combination
of flavorful, nutritious ingredients. Served as a main dish,
this savory combination hits the mark as a light, succulent
one-dish meal. Of course, you can substitute the turkey
with chicken, pork, fish, other vegetables, or beef. As
another variation, substitute Mexican Tomato Sauce
(#17) for the Pasilla Chile Sauce. For extra flavor, sprinkle each serving with 1 tablespoon grated lowfat cheese.

nonstick pan coating
½ pound extra-lean turkey, skinned, boned, and cut
  into small tenderloin pieces
1 small white onion, finely sliced into rings
½ cup green onions, finely sliced
1 to 2 cloves garlic, crushed in a garlic press
⅛ to 1 fresh serrano or jalapeño chile, seeded,
  washed, and finely sliced (optional, for a
  spicier dish)
1 fresh anaheim chile, seeded, washed, and
  finely sliced
1 cup celery, finely sliced
1½ cups mushrooms, sliced
2 cups Pasilla Chile Sauce (Recipe #20)
1 teaspoon fresh thyme, minced
5 ounces vermicelli noodles, cooked
salt and freshly ground pepper

Spray a large skillet with nonstick pan coating and over medium-high heat. Evenly brown the turkey t in the juices; turn frequently. Add the white and gre onions, garlic, serrano and anaheim chiles, and celer Sauté the turkey and onion mixture for 3 minutes; sti frequently. Stir in mushrooms; reduce heat to low. M remaining ingredients, excluding the noodles. Cover; cook the mixture for 4 minutes. Stir in the cooked noodles; combine well. Salt and pepper the vermicelli dish according to individual taste. Serve the hot dish immediately.

Serves 6

Each serving provides:

177	Calories	26 g	Carbohydrate
16 g	Protein	65 mg	Sodium
1 g	Fat	24 mg	Cholesterol

81

—❦—

Spanish Chicken and Rice

(Arroz con Pollo)

Preparation time: 15 minutes
Cooking time: 20 to 25 minutes

The Spaniards brought this classic chicken casserole to
the shores of Mexico. Prepared in one skillet, this easy-to-
make meal is a delightful blend of chicken, rice, and
Mexican Tomato Sauce. Serve this casserole with a small
side dish of beans and a salad to create a brilliantly colored, high-powered protein meal for your family and
friends.

nonstick pan coating
2 cups extra-lean chicken, skinned, boned,
      and cut into large tenderloin pieces
2 small white onions, sliced into rings
1/2 cup green onions, finely sliced
1 to 2 cloves garlic, crushed in a garlic press
1 fresh anaheim chile, seeded, washed and
      finely chopped
1/8 to 1 fresh serrano or jalapeño chile, seeded,
      washed, and finely chopped (optional, for
      a spicier dish)
1 cup bell peppers, seeded, washed, and chopped
4 medium ripe tomatoes, blanched or roasted,
      peeled, and finely chopped
1/2 cup long-grain rice, uncooked
1/2 cup low-salt broth
1 1/2 cups water

1 teaspoon fresh oregano, minced
1 bay leaf
6 sprigs fresh cilantro
salt and freshly ground pepper

Spray a large skillet with nonstick pan coating and heat
over medium-high heat. Evenly brown the chicken to sear
in the juices; turn frequently. Add the white and green
onions, garlic, anaheim and serrano chiles, and bell peppers. Sauté the chicken and onion mixture until the
onions become tender; stir frequently. Stir in the tomatoes. Cook the chicken and onion mixture for 2 minutes;
reduce heat to low.

Add remaining ingredients, excluding the sprigs of
cilantro. Cover; simmer the chicken and onion mixture
for 20 to 25 minutes until the rice is tender and absorbs
the liquid. Add more boiling water, 1/4 cup at a time, if the
water cooks away. Remove the bay leaf. Salt and pepper
the dish according to individual taste. Serve the hot
chicken dish garnished with fresh cilantro sprigs.

Serves 6

Each serving provides:

195	Calories	42 g	Carbohydrate
31 g	Protein	85 mg	Sodium
2 g	Fat	64 mg	Cholesterol

82

—❧—

Chicken Stew

(*Guisado de Pollo*)

Preparation time: 15 minutes
Cooking time: 15 to 20 minutes

This robust stew, savory with the flavor of chicken and
vegetables, offers both a satisfying dinner and nourish-
ment. A meal in itself, this stew is perfect for an informal
meal on a cold or rainy day. To top the meal off, serve this
dish with a fresh garden salad.

nonstick pan coating
2 cups extra-lean chicken, skinned, boned, and cut
    into large tenderloin pieces
2 small white onions, sliced into rings
1/2 cup green onions, finely sliced
1 to 2 cloves garlic, crushed in a garlic press
1 anaheim chile, seeded, washed, and finely chopped
1/8 to 1 fresh serrano or jalapeño chile, seeded,
    washed, and finely chopped (optional, for a
    spicier dish)
1 cup celery, chopped
2 medium ripe tomatoes, blanched or roasted,
    peeled, and chopped
3/4 cup long-grain rice, cooked
2 cups water
1 teaspoon oregano, minced
2 bay leaves
6 sprigs fresh cilantro
salt and freshly ground pepper

Spray a large skillet with nonstick pan coating and heat over medium-high heat. Evenly brown the chicken to sear in the juices; turn frequently. Add the white and green onions, garlic, anaheim and serrano chiles, and celery. Sauté the chicken and onion mixture until the white onions become tender; stir frequently. Reduce heat to medium-low.

Add the remaining ingredients, excluding the sprigs of cilantro. The liquid should cover the chicken mixture by 1/2 inch in the skillet. Cover; simmer the chicken and onion mixture for 15 to 20 minutes until the chicken becomes tender. Remove the bay leaves. Salt and pepper the stew according to individual taste. Serve the stew from a tureen garnished with fresh cilantro sprigs.

Serves 7

Each serving provides:

182	Calories	39 g	Carbohydrate
43 g	Protein	85 mg	Sodium
2 g	Fat	55 mg	Cholesterol

83

Breasts of Chicken in Green Chile Sauce

(Pechugas de Pollo en Chile Verde)

Preparation time: 15 minutes
Baking time: 40 to 45 minutes
Preheat oven to 350°

Here is a simple and attractive way to prepare chicken
breasts. Fresh Green Chile Sauce brings out the mellow
taste of the baked chicken to tangy perfection. Serve the
baked chicken with rice, vermicelli, or a vegetable side
dish for a complete meal. For a more formal dinner, serve
the baked chicken on a bed of fluffy cooked rice with
fresh cilantro sprigs and chopped green onions as garnish.

nonstick pan coating
1¹/₂ pounds extra-lean chicken breasts, skinned
    and boned
1 small white onion, sliced in rings
1 cup mushrooms, finely sliced
¹/₂ cup green onions, finely minced
1 to 2 cloves garlic, crushed in a garlic press
2 cups Green Chile Sauce (Recipe #15)
1 cup low-salt broth
1 teaspoon fresh oregano, minced
salt and freshly ground pepper

Spray a large skillet with nonstick pan coating and heat
over medium-high heat. Evenly brown the chicken pieces
to sear in the juices. Place the chicken in a large, ungreased

casserole with a lid. Combine the remaining ingredients in a medium-size bowl. Smother the chicken pieces with the onion and Green Chile Sauce mixture from the bowl. Cover; bake the chicken in preheated oven for 40 to 45 minutes. The chicken is done when it cooks thoroughly and pulls apart with a fork. Salt and pepper the chicken dish according to individual taste. Serve the hot chicken casserole immediately.

Serves 6

Each serving provides:

182	Calories	38 g	Carbohydrate
43 g	Protein	109 mg	Sodium
3 g	Fat	96 mg	Cholesterol

84

—❧—

Grilled Chicken

(Pollo Asada)

Preparation time: 10 minutes
Refrigeration time: 20 minutes
Grilling time: 10 to 12 minutes

Grilled lean chicken is an appealing way to serve a tasty,
lowfat meal. A tangy marinade of lime juice adds a distinctive zing to the flavor of the extra-lean chicken pieces.
This spicy, grilled chicken dish tastes even more delicious
when served with a crisp tossed salad and vermicelli or
rice. For a more elegant dinner, serve the grilled chicken
pieces on a bed of fluffy, cooked rice surrounded by fresh
or wilted spinach leaves. If you cannot grill outdoors, you
can also broil these pieces of chicken 4 to 5 inches under
the broiler or in a cast-iron grill pan.

1/3 cup Green Chile Sauce (Recipe #15)
2 tablespoons lime juice
1 1/2 pounds extra-lean chicken, skinned, boned,
    and cut into tenderloin pieces
1 medium white onion, halved and finely sliced
1 cup green onions, finely sliced
1 to 2 cloves garlic, crushed in a garlic press
1/8 to 1 fresh serrano or jalapeño chile, seeded,
    washed, and finely chopped (optional, for
    a spicier dish)
1 fresh anaheim chile, seeded, washed, and
    finely chopped
1 medium tomato, blanched or roasted,
    seeded, and finely chopped

6 sprigs fresh cilantro
salt and freshly ground pepper

Combine the Green Chile Sauce and lime juice in a large
glass baking dish. Rub the chicken in the marinade to
thoroughly coat the chicken with the juices. Cover and
marinate the chicken in the refrigerator for 20 minutes;
turn occasionally.

Sauté the remaining ingredients, excluding the tomato and cilantro, with 2 tablespoons of water in a saucepan over medium-high heat until the white onions become
tender; reduce heat to low. Add tomato; cook for 2 minutes. Salt and pepper the onion and tomato mixture
according to individual taste.

Remove the chicken from marinade; reserve the
marinade. Grill the chicken for 5 to 6 minutes on each
side over hot coals; occasionally brush the chicken with
the remaining marinade. Grill chicken until it becomes
tender and cooked white on the inside. Attractively align
the grilled chicken on six oven-warmed plates. Spoon the
onion and tomato mixture down the center of the grilled
chicken. Garnish each plate of chicken with fresh cilantro
sprigs. Serve the hot chicken dish immediately.

Serves 6

Each serving provides:

183	Calories	39 g	Carbohydrate
43 g	Protein	108 mg	Sodium
3 g	Fat	96 mg	Cholesterol

85

—✎—

Grilled Chicken Strips

(Fajitas de Pollo)

Preparation time: 10 minutes
Refrigeration time: 1 hour
Grilling time: 16 to 22 minutes
Preheat oven to 350°

Chicken *fajitas* are a festive way to entertain your friends
with a delicious and exotic feast. You will enjoy the strips
of grilled chicken and sautéed vegetables wrapped in soft,
warm flour tortillas. In Mexico, this same recipe is popular and similarly served with strips of marinated steak. To
complete this exquisite feast, place small serving bowls of
shredded lettuce, chopped tomatoes, jalapeño chiles,
salsa, and lowfat sour cream on the table as condiments
for do-it-yourself stuffing. If you cannot grill outdoors,
broil the chicken strips 4 to 5 inches under the broiler or
in a cast-iron grill pan.

2 tablespoons lime juice
1 tablespoon cider vinegar
1¼ pounds extra-lean chicken, skinned, boned,
    and cut into tenderloin pieces
6 fresh lowfat flour tortillas (6-inch)
1 medium white onion, halved and finely sliced
1 cup green onions, finely sliced
1 to 2 cloves garlic, crushed in a garlic press
1 cup fresh mushrooms, finely sliced
1 medium red bell pepper, seeded, washed, halved,
    and finely sliced
⅛ to 1 fresh serrano or jalapeño chile, seeded, washed,
    and finely chopped (optional, for a spicier dish)

1 fresh anaheim chile, seeded, washed, and
    finely chopped
2 to 4 sprigs fresh cilantro, minced
salt and freshly ground pepper

Combine the lime juice and cider vinegar in a large glass
baking dish. Rub the chicken in the marinade to thoroughly coat the chicken. Cover and marinate the chicken
in the refrigerator for 1 hour; turn the chicken pieces
occasionally.

Wrap flour tortillas in foil. Warm in preheated oven
about 10 minutes, until tortillas are soft. Remove the flour
tortillas from the oven and set them, wrapped in foil, aside.

Sauté the remaining ingredients, excluding the
minced cilantro, with 2 tablespoons of water in a saucepan over medium-high heat until the white onions become
tender; reduce heat to low. Remove chicken from marinade; reserve the marinade. Grill chicken strips for 8 to
11 minutes on each side until they become tender and
cooked white on the inside. Occasionally brush the chick-
en with the remaining marinade.

Place the grilled chicken on an oven-warmed platter.
Garnish with fresh cilantro. Place the flour tortillas,
wrapped in foil, in a basket to keep warm. Place the
sautéed onion and chile mixture in a small serving bowl.

To eat the fajitas, lay open a tortilla and spoon a portion of the chicken and the onion and chile mixture down
the center of each tortilla. Add the additional condiments.
Fold the flour tortilla in half or roll it together like a burrito.

Serves 6

Each serving provides:

224	Calories	48 g	Carbohydrate
38 g	Protein	116 mg	Sodium
3 g	Fat	80 mg	Cholesterol

86

—❦—

Stuffed Chiles with Turkey

(Chiles Rellenos de Pavo)

Preparation time: 20 minutes
Baking time: 10 minutes
Preheat oven to 350°

Mexicans like to stuff their chiles in a variety of ways
with a variety of ingredients. For a change, you can
replace the turkey with extra-lean chicken, beef, or pork.
To complete your meal, serve the stuffed chiles with a side
dish of beans and a crisp salad or vegetables. For extra
flavor, lightly sprinkle the tops of the stuffed chiles with
grated sweet corn, lowfat Jack, or Parmesan cheese.

6 large fresh poblano or anaheim chiles
nonstick pan coating
1 pound extra-lean turkey breast, cut into
    1½ inch cubes
1 medium white onion, chopped
½ cup green onions, finely sliced
1 to 2 cloves garlic, crushed in a garlic press
⅛ to 1 fresh serrano or jalapeño chile, seeded,
    washed, and finely chopped (optional, for
    a spicier dish)
1 cup Green Chile Sauce (Recipe #15)
½ cup long-grain rice, cooked
2 teaspoons lime juice
1 teaspoon fresh oregano, minced
1 teaspoon fresh thyme, minced
nonstick pan coating
salt and freshly ground pepper

Preheat the broiler. Roast the poblano or anaheim chiles 2 to 3 inches under the broiler for 3 to 4 minutes on each side. Occasionally rotate the chiles until they evenly brown and blister on each side. Put the chiles in a tightly closed plastic bag to steam for 5 minutes. Carefully peel off the charred skin. Leaving the stem intact, carefully slit the top of each chile. Rinse and seed the chiles; set aside.

Spray a large skillet with nonstick pan coating and heat over medium-high heat. Evenly brown the turkey to sear in the juices; turn frequently. Stir in the white and green onions, garlic, and serrano chile. Sauté the turkey and onion mixture until the onions become tender; stir frequently. Stir in remaining ingredients; turn heat off. Salt and pepper the dish according to individual taste.

Evenly spray a baking sheet with nonstick pan coating, entirely covering the surface so chiles will not stick. Carefully stuff each poblano or anaheim chile with the cooked turkey and onion mixture. Place each stuffed chile on the prepared baking sheet. Bake the stuffed chiles in preheated oven for 10 minutes. Serve the hot stuffed chiles immediately.

Serves 6

Each serving provides:

197	Calories	21 g	Carbohydrate
26 g	Protein	65 mg	Sodium
1 g	Fat	49 mg	Cholesterol

87

❧

Mexican-style Chicken
(Picadillo de Pollo)

Preparation time: 15 minutes
Cooking time: 15 to 20 minutes

Here is an all-purpose filling or stuffing for burritos, chiles, tostadas, enchiladas, or soft tacos. For variation, substitute leftover seafood, turkey, or pork for the chicken. Increase the amount of tomatoes and Mexican Tomato Sauce in this recipe, if you prefer a piquant, Mexican-style spaghetti dish served over hot spaghetti noodles. Add a fresh garden salad and a crusty piece of French bread to create the perfect, spicy meal.

nonstick pan coating
1 pound extra-lean chicken, skinned, boned, and
    cut into tenderloin pieces
1 small white onion, chopped
1/2 cup green onions, finely sliced
1 to 2 cloves garlic, crushed in a garlic press
1/8 to 1 fresh serrano or jalapeño chile, seeded, washed,
    and finely chopped (optional, for a spicier dish)
1 fresh anaheim or poblano chile, seeded, washed,
    and finely chopped
1 cup fresh mushrooms, sliced
1 cup Mexican Tomato Sauce (Recipe #17)
2 medium ripe tomatoes, blanched or roasted,
    peeled, and chopped
1 tablespoon lime juice
1 teaspoon fresh oregano, minced

1 teaspoon fresh thyme, minced
salt and freshly ground pepper

Spray a 5-quart pot with nonstick pan coating and heat over medium-high heat. Evenly brown the chicken to sear in the juices; turn frequently. Add the white and green onions, garlic, and serrano and anaheim chiles. Cook the mixture until the onions become tender. Mix in the remaining ingredients; reduce heat to low. Cover; simmer the mixture gently for 15 to 20 minutes, stir occasionally. Add salt and pepper according to individual taste. Serve the hot chicken dish immediately.

Serves 6

Each serving provides:

140	Calories	29 g	Carbohydrate
30 g	Protein	71 mg	Sodium
2 g	Fat	64 mg	Cholesterol

88

❦

Chicken in Red Chile Sauce
(Pollo en Salsa de Chile Rojo)

Preparation time: 15 minutes
Cooking time: 20 to 25 minutes

Beef, pork, or chicken dishes, smothered in rich, savory
chile sauces, are very popular throughout Mexico and
may be found hot and bubbling in large pots in most
Mexican restaurants or street cafes. Here is a quick and
easy way to prepare this very saucy chicken dish. As a
variation to this recipe, cut the chicken into smaller
1-inch cubes to serve in burritos, chimichangas, enchiladas, tostadas, or tacos.

nonstick pan coating
1½ pound extra-lean chicken, skinned, boned, and
        cut into tenderloin pieces
1 medium white onion, cut into ½-inch slices
½ cup green onions, finely sliced
1 to 2 cloves garlic, crushed in a garlic press
⅛ to 1 fresh serrano or jalapeño chile, seeded,
    washed, and finely chopped (optional, for a
    spicier dish)
2½ cups Red Chile Sauce (Recipe #16)
1 teaspoon fresh oregano, minced
6 sprigs fresh cilantro
salt and freshly ground pepper

Spray a large skillet with nonstick pan coating and heat
over medium-high heat. Evenly brown the chicken to sear
in the juices; turn frequently. Stir in the white and green

onions, garlic, and serrano chile. Sauté the chicken and onion mixture until the onions become tender; stir frequently. Stir in the remaining ingredients, excluding the sprigs of cilantro. Cover; simmer the chicken and onion mixture for 20 to 25 minutes, until the chicken cooks thoroughly and pulls apart with a fork. Salt and pepper the dish according to individual taste. Garnish each serving with fresh cilantro sprigs.

Serves 6

Each serving provides:

186	Calories	39 g	Carbohydrate
43 g	Protein	110 mg	Sodium
3 g	Fat	96 mg	Cholesterol

89

❦

Pineapple Chicken
(Pollo con Piña)

Preparation time: 15 minutes
Baking time: 40 to 45 minutes

There is nothing like a dazzling combination of succulent pineapple and chicken as presented in this recipe. Serve this dish with or over Mexican Green Rice (#57) and a tropical fruit salad for a festive culinary celebration. You might want to use lean turkey as an alternative to the chicken.

1 fresh anaheim or poblano chile
nonstick pan coating
1 pound extra-lean chicken or small chicken breasts
    (6 pieces), skinned, boned, and cut into
    tenderloin pieces
1 small white onion, chopped
$^1/_2$ cup green onions, finely sliced
1 to 2 cloves garlic, crushed in a garlic press
$^1/_8$ to 1 fresh serrano or jalapeño chile, seeded,
    washed, and finely chopped (optional, for
    a spicier dish)
1 cup Mexican Tomato Sauce (Recipe #17)
$^1/_2$ cup low-salt broth
$1^1/_2$ cups pineapple juice
1 cup pineapple, chopped in $1^1/_2$-inch pieces
$^1/_2$ cup snow peas
1 small ripe tomato, blanched or roasted,
    peeled, and chopped
1 cup fresh mushrooms, sliced

1 teaspoon fresh oregano, minced
1 bay leaf
1 teaspoon fresh thyme, minced
3 to 6 sprigs fresh cilantro, minced (optional)
salt and freshly ground pepper

Preheat the broiler. Roast the anaheim chile 2 to 3 inches under the broiler for 3 to 4 minutes on each side. Occasionally, rotate the chile until it evenly browns and blisters on each side. Put the chile in a tightly closed plastic bag to steam for 5 minutes. Carefully peel off the charred skin. Cut off the stem, seed, rinse, and finely chop the chile; set aside.

Spray a large skillet with nonstick coating and heat over medium-high heat. Evenly brown the chicken pieces to sear in the juices. Place the chicken pieces into an ungreased, glass baking dish. Sauté the white and green onions, garlic, and anaheim and serrano chile in a large skillet with 2 tablespoons of water over medium heat until the onions become tender; stir frequently. Mix in the remaining ingredients, excluding the cilantro sprigs. Salt and pepper the dish according to individual taste.

Pour sauce mixture over the chicken in the casserole dish. Bake the chicken in a 350° oven for 40 to 45 minutes until the chicken cooks thoroughly and pulls apart with a fork. Remove the bay leaf. Sprinkle fresh minced cilantro over the chicken. Serve the hot chicken dish immediately.

Serves 6

Each serving provides:

187	Calories	49 g	Carbohydrate
30 g	Protein	85 mg	Sodium
2 g	Fat	64 mg	Cholesterol

Mexican Seafood Dishes

Mexican seafood dishes are not well known in America. Nevertheless, the combination of chiles and seafood is a rare blend of savory, exotic flavors. Mexico has six thousand miles of coastline on both the east and west coast of the country, bordering the Pacific and Caribbean oceans and the Gulf of Mexico. Early in the sixteenth century, the Spanish wrote of the beauty and bounty of fresh fish and shellfish discovered along the coast of Mexico. At the time, Montezuma, the Aztec emperor, often sent runners to the ocean to bring back shrimp or his favorite fish. Today, many regional seafood specialties are famous throughout Mexico. Snapper, shrimp, shark, marlin, squid, swordfish, sea bass, and tuna are just a sampling of the mesmerizing array of fish and seafood common throughout Mexico. In addition, there is a vast variety of fish not commonly known in America. The fishing industry is alive and well in Mexico. Fishermen export much of their catch to Americans who eagerly await the abundance provided by Mexican waters.

Fresh, healthy fish is by far the best source of lean, complete protein high in vitamins and minerals and low in saturated fat and cholesterol. Versatile, affordable, and quick-cooking, fish is increasingly popular in America. Saturated fat concentrates in the skin of the fish. Without the skin, 90 percent of the calories are from protein and 10 percent of the calories are from fat. Fish also contains high amounts of omega 3 fatty acids. Reports show that these acids lower blood pressure, cut cholesterol, and reduce the risk of heart attack.

The recipes in *Mexican Seafood Dishes* present an array of delicious, simple, spicy seafood dishes blended with the enticing flavors of herbs, chiles, and other vegetables. Regional specialties, popular throughout Mexico, uniquely blend a common variety of fresh vegetables, fruits, and chiles. Most of these dishes reflect the culinary influences of both Spain and the native Indians. Fruits and spicy chiles add a distinctive, desirable zest to the milder flavors of a variety of seafood. For great flavor and texture, always cook fish fresh and for as short a time as possible. The short cooking time leaves the succulent flavors in the flesh, without drying it out.

Using fish and shellfish commonly found in the United States, this section attempts to give the health-conscious cook a memorable array of tantalizing seafood dishes. Each dish is low in calories and fat and will enhance your unique culinary palette of recipes with exotic gifts from the sea.

Mexican Seafood Dishes

90

—⚜—

Fresh Fish Appetizer
(Ceviche)

Preparation time: 15 minutes
Refrigeration time: 3 hours

The words "fresh and zesty" perfectly describe this famous Mexican appetizer. It hardly seems possible that this exquisite dish is so simple to prepare. The fresh fish pieces literally cook in the lime juice for several hours to absorb the penetrating citrus fruit flavors blended with the mild chile salsa. Your culinary flair will impress your family and guests when you serve this exotic dish as a dazzling prelude to an elegant dinner.

¹/₂ pound fresh sole fillets, cut into 2¹/₂-inch pieces
¹/₃ cup lime juice
8 sprigs fresh cilantro
1 small white onion, finely sliced
¹/₃ cup green onions, finely sliced
1 to 2 cloves garlic, crushed in a garlic press
¹/₈ to 1 fresh serrano or jalapeño chile, seeded,
        washed, and finely chopped (optional, for
        a spicier dish)
2 medium ripe tomatoes, diced
salt and freshly ground pepper

Place the pieces of sole and lime juice in a rectangular, ungreased casserole dish. Rub the sole in the lime marinade to thoroughly coat the fish with the juices. Refrigerate the marinade for at least 3 hours; occasionally turn the fish.

Mince 2 sprigs of cilantro; set aside. Sauté the white and green onions, garlic, and serrano chile with 1 tablespoon of water in a medium-size skillet over medium-high heat; stir frequently. Cook the mixture until the onions become tender; remove the skillet from the burner. Mix together the tomatoes, 2 sprigs minced cilantro, and the sautéed onion mixture in a medium-size bowl. Refrigerate the tomato and onion mixture for 30 minutes. Salt and pepper the dish according to individual taste.

Spread one-sixth portion of the tomato and onion mixture in the center of six cold small plates; set aside. Drain the pieces of sole; reserve the lime marinade. Attractively arrange the pieces of sole in the shape of a star on top of the tomato and onion mixture on each plate. Drizzle the remaining lime marinade across the individual pieces of sole. Garnish each plate, in the center of the star, with the remaining fresh cilantro sprigs.

Serves 6

Each serving provides:

58	Calories	6 g	Carbohydrate
8 g	Protein	41 mg	Sodium
1 g	Fat	18 mg	Cholesterol

91

❧

Mexican-style Grilled Shrimp

(Camarón Asada)

Preparation time: 20 minutes
Refrigeration time: 1 hour
Grilling Time: 5 minutes

This succulent, piquant shrimp dish aptly demonstrates the tasty combination of shrimp and chiles. Quickly grilled over hot coals, you can serve this super-easy-to-prepare dish within minutes. If you cannot grill outdoors, you can broil the shrimp 4 to 5 inches under the broiler or in a cast-iron grill pan. Make sure you turn the shrimp 2 or 3 times while cooking. Add the seeds of the anaheim chile or a small jalapeño to enhance the spicy flavor of this attractive dish. A fresh fruit salad and an appetizing noodle or rice side dish will pleasantly complement an appealing seafood meal.

¼ cup tequila (optional)
¼ cup apple cider vinegar
⅓ cup lime juice
18 fresh raw jumbo shrimp (1 pound), peeled,
    deveined, cleaned, and without the tails
18 small ripe cherry tomatoes
1 small yellow bell pepper, seeded, washed, and
    cut into 9 slices (2-inch-wide)
1 small green bell pepper, seeded, washed, and cut
    into 9 slices (2-inch-wide)
18 small fresh mushroom caps
1 small white onion, quartered
½ cup green onions, finely sliced

1 to 2 cloves garlic, crushed in a garlic press
1 fresh anaheim or poblano chile, seeded, washed,
    and chopped
1/8 to 1 fresh serrano or jalapeño chile, seeded,
    washed, and finely chopped (optional, for
    a spicier dish)
1 to 3 sprigs fresh cilantro, minced
salt and freshly ground pepper

Combine the tequila, apple cider vinegar and lime juice in
a large glass baking dish. Rub the shrimp, tomatoes, yellow and green bell peppers, and mushroom caps in the
marinade to thoroughly coat the pieces. Cover; marinate
the shrimp mixture in the refrigerator for 1 hour.

Remove the shrimp and other ingredients from marinade; reserve the marinade. Alternately skewer 3 shrimp,
3 cherry tomatoes, 3 pieces of bell pepper, and 3 mushroom caps on 6 metal skewers; set aside.

Sauté the white and green onions, garlic, anaheim
and serrano chiles, and cilantro with 2 tablespoons of
water in a saucepan over medium-high heat until the
onions become tender; reduce heat to low; stir frequently.

Grill the skewered shrimp and vegetables for 5 minutes over hot coals until the shrimp turns pink; turn two
or three times. Occasionally brush the skewered shrimp
and vegetables with the marinade. Add the remaining
marinade to the onion mixture; cook 2 minutes. Salt and
pepper to taste. Place 1/6 portion of the onion mixture on
six oven-warmed plates. Set each skewer of shrimp across
the bed of onions on each plate. Serve the hot grilled
shrimp immediately.

Serves 6

Each serving provides:

140	Calories	10 g	Carbohydrate
17 g	Protein	125 mg	Sodium
2 g	Fat	115 mg	Cholesterol

92

---✦---

Red Snapper Veracruz

(Huachinango a la Veracruzana)

Preparation time: 15 minutes
Refrigeration time: 30 minutes
Cooking time: 20 minutes

This popular regional specialty dish from Veracruz is very simple to prepare, colorful, and succulent. You can substitute the red snapper with any similar firm white fish like cod, pike, or halibut. Serve this attractive dish with a flavorful rice or vegetable side dish to enliven this elegant, mouth-watering recipe.

2 fresh anaheim chiles
6 medium fresh red snapper fillets, skinned, and
        boned (2 pounds)
3 tablespoons lime juice
1 small white onion, finely chopped
1/4 cup green onions, finely sliced
1 to 2 cloves garlic, crushed in a garlic press
1/8 to 1 fresh serrano or jalapeño chile, seeded,
        washed, and finely chopped (optional, for
        a spicier dish)
1 small ripe tomato, finely chopped
2 cups Mexican Tomato Sauce (Recipe #17)
6 sprigs fresh cilantro (optional)
salt and freshly ground pepper

Preheat the broiler. Roast the anaheim chiles 2 to 3 inches under the broiler for 3 to 4 minutes on each side. Occasionally rotate the chiles until they evenly brown and blister on each side. Put the chiles in a tightly closed plastic bag to steam for 5 minutes. Carefully peel off the charred skin. Cut off the stems, seed, rinse, and finely chop; set aside.

Rinse the fish in cold water. Gently prick both sides of the fish with a fork. Put 2 tablespoons of lime juice in a large, ungreased casserole dish. Rub the fillets on both sides in the marinade. Refrigerate the fish in the marinade for 30 minutes; drain the marinade. Bake the fish on a baking rack in a 350° oven for 20 minutes. The fish is done when it flakes apart with a fork.

Sauté the white and green onions, garlic, anaheim and serrano chiles, and the remaining 1 tablespoon of lime juice in a medium-size skillet over medium-high heat until the onions become tender; stir frequently. Add the tomato; cook for 2 minutes. Mix in the Mexican Tomato Sauce; reduce the heat to low.

Arrange the baked fish fillets on a large serving platter. Attractively cover the fillets with the onion and Mexican Tomato Sauce mixture. Salt and pepper the dish according to individual taste. Garnish the platter with fresh cilantro sprigs.

Serves 6

Each serving provides:

179	Calories	9 g	Carbohydrate
30 g	Protein	138 mg	Sodium
2 g	Fat	72 mg	Cholesterol

93

⎯⎯❦⎯⎯

Sea Scallops in
Spicy Red Sauce

(Mariscos en Salsa de Chile Rojo)

Preparation time: 15 minutes
Refrigeration time: 30 minutes
Cooking time: 15 to 20 minutes

Why serve another ordinary meal when you can make a
stir with this savory, eye-appealing meal of scallops slowly simmered in a thick, spicy red chile sauce. Very fresh,
firm, large sea scallops are best for this light and lively
seafood dish. Serve the luscious scallops with rice and a
garden-fresh salad to create an appetizing meal. For a
more elegant dinner, serve the scallops on a platter atop a
bed of vermicelli or fettucine noodles, cooked al dente,
surrounded by a ring of fresh or wilted spinach leaves.

1 pound large, fresh sea scallops
$1/2$ cup white wine
1 medium-size white onion, chopped
$1/2$ cup green onions, finely sliced
1 to 2 cloves garlic, crushed in a garlic press
1 cup green bell peppers, quartered, seeded, washed,
    and thinly sliced
2 medium ripe tomatoes, blanched or roasted,
    peeled, and chopped
1 cup fresh mushrooms, sliced
1 cup Mexican Tomato Sauce (Recipe #17)
1 cup Red Chile Sauce (Recipe #16)
1 teaspoon fresh oregano, minced

1 bay leaf
1 teaspoon fresh thyme, minced
6 sprigs fresh cilantro
salt and freshly ground pepper

Rinse the scallops in cold water. Place the scallops and
wine in an ungreased, glass baking dish. Rub the scallops
in the wine marinade to thoroughly coat the scallops.
Refrigerate the scallops in the marinade for 30 minutes;
turn the scallops occasionally.

Sauté the white and green onions, garlic, and bell
peppers with 2 tablespoons of water in a large skillet over
medium-high heat until the onions become tender. Add
the tomatoes; cook for 2 minutes. Stir in the scallops,
marinade, and remaining ingredients, excluding the
cilantro sprigs. Reduce heat to low and cover. Simmer the
scallops for 15 to 20 minutes; stir the mixture occasionally. Remove the bay leaf. Salt and pepper the dish according to individual taste. Serve the hot scallop dish immediately. Garnish with fresh cilantro sprigs.

Serves 6

Each serving provides:

133	Calories	13 g	Carbohydrate
15 g	Protein	140 mg	Sodium
1 g	Fat	25 mg	Cholesterol

94

—✦—

Mexican-style Trout
(Trucha a la Mexicana)

Preparation time: 15 minutes
Refrigeration time: 15 minutes
Baking time: 20 minutes
Preheat oven to 350°

Here is an especially quick and simple way to prepare a light and festive-looking meal ideal for a summer party outdoors on your patio. Combined with the flavors and colors of Mexico, this trout recipe subtly blends the flavors of trout, chiles, mushrooms, and spinach. Cook the fish just until the flesh easily flakes when pulled apart with a fork. For variation, try grilling the trout wrapped in foil over a bed of hot coals. For an entire meal, serve these trout fillets with a side dish of potatoes or rice and a fresh salad. For a more formal occasion, serve the trout fillets over a bed of rice on an oven-warmed platter.

6 small, fresh trout fillets, skinned and cleaned
    (about 1³/₄ pounds)
¹/₃ cup white wine
1 tablespoon lime juice
1 bunch spinach (about 3 cups), thoroughly cleaned
1 cup fresh mushrooms, sliced
1 small white onion, chopped
¹/₂ cup green onions, finely sliced
1 to 2 cloves garlic, crushed in a garlic press
¹/₈ to 1 fresh serrano or jalapeño chile, seeded,
    washed, and finely chopped (optional, for
    a spicier dish)

³/₄ cup Green Chile Sauce (Recipe #15)
6 small cherry tomatoes
6 sprigs fresh cilantro, minced (optional)
salt and freshly ground pepper

Clean the trout fillets in cold water. Gently prick both sides of the trout with a fork. Put the wine and lime juice in an ungreased, glass baking dish. Rub the fillets on both sides in the marinade. Refrigerate the trout in the marinade for 15 minutes. Drain the marinade from the trout; reserve the marinade. Bake the trout on a baking rack in preheated oven for 20 minutes. The trout fillets are done when they flake apart with a fork.

Place a steamer basket inside a 5-quart pot. Bring 1 inch of water in the pot to the boiling point. Reduce heat to low. Place the spinach and mushrooms into the pot on the steamer basket. Cook the vegetables, partially covered, about 5 minutes until just tender.

Sauté the reserved marinade, white and green onions, garlic, and chile over medium-high heat in a medium-size saucepan until the onions become tender; stir frequently. Add the spinach, mushrooms, and Green Chile Sauce; reduce heat to low. Salt and pepper the dish according to individual taste. Remove the fish from the oven to arrange each trout on six oven-warmed plates. Decoratively cover the trout horizontally across the center with the sautéed onion and spinach mixture. Garnish each plate with cherry tomatoes and fresh minced cilantro.

Serves 6

Each serving provides:

164	Calories	7 g	Carbohydrate
27 g	Protein	160 mg	Sodium
2 g	Fat	63 mg	Cholesterol

95

— ❧ —

Sea Scallops in
White Wine Sauce

(Mariscos en Vino Blanco)

Preparation time: 15 minutes
Refrigeration time: 30 minutes
Cooking time: 10 to 15 minutes

This seafood dish is an interesting combination of delicate flavors and exquisite aromas. Served over a bed of fluffy rice or vermicelli noodles cooked al dente, this is an incredibly succulent and fulfilling meal. Very fresh, firm sea scallops are best for this light, elegant recipe where the soaked sea scallops simmer in a savory wine sauce. After trying this recipe, you will have greater appreciation for the versatility and distinct blended flavor of fresh scallops and chiles. For variation, try this delicious treat served over a bed of garden-fresh or wilted spinach leaves garnished with lots of freshly ground peppercorns. It's heavenly!

1 to 2 fresh anaheim or poblano chiles
1 pound fresh scallops
⅓ cup white wine
1 tablespoon lime juice
1 cup bell peppers, halved, seeded, washed, and sliced
1 medium white onion, chopped or finely sliced
½ cup green onions, finely sliced
1 to 2 cloves garlic, crushed in a garlic press
1 cup fresh mushrooms, sliced
⅛ to 1 fresh serrano or jalapeño chile, seeded, washed,
    and finely chopped (optional, for a spicier dish)

1½ cups low-salt broth
1½ teaspoons fresh oregano, minced
2 sprigs fresh cilantro, minced
1 bay leaf
1 teaspoon fresh thyme, minced
salt and freshly ground pepper

Preheat the broiler. Roast the anaheim chiles 2 to 3 inches under the broiler for 3 to 4 minutes on each side. Occasionally rotate the chiles until they evenly brown and blister on each side. Put the chiles in a tightly closed plastic bag to steam for 5 minutes. Carefully peel off the charred skin. Cut off the stem, seed, rinse, and finely chop; set aside.

Clean the scallops in cold water. Place the scallops, wine, and lime juice in an ungreased, glass baking dish. Rub the scallops to thoroughly coat them in the marinade. Refrigerate the scallops in the marinade for 30 minutes. Sauté the scallops, bell peppers, and marinade in a large skillet over medium heat for 3 minutes; stir frequently. Stir in the white and green onions, garlic, mushrooms, and serrano and anaheim chiles. Cook the scallop and onion mixture until the onions become tender; stir frequently. Stir in the remaining ingredients; reduce heat to low. Cover; simmer the scallop dish for 10 to 15 minutes; stir frequently. Salt and pepper the dish according to individual taste. Remove the bay leaf before serving. Serve the hot scallop dish immediately.

Serves 6

Each serving provides:

107	Calories	9 g	Carbohydrate
14 g	Protein	131 mg	Sodium
1 g	Fat	25 mg	Cholesterol

96

❧

Baked Fish in White Wine Sauce

(Pescado en Vino Blanco)

Preparation time: 20 minutes
Refrigeration time: 30 minutes
Baking time: 20 minutes
Preheat oven to 350°

This appetizing fish recipe features white fish fillets baked
in the blended juices of wine and chiles. You can easily
adapt this classic baked-fish recipe to include most firm,
white fish fillets, including sole, halibut, cod, red snapper,
or perch. Serve this simple dish with a side dish of potatoes or rice and a garden-fresh dinner salad.

6 small, firm, white fish fillets, cleaned and
        skinned (2 pounds)
½ cup white wine
3 tablespoons lime juice
2 fresh anaheim chiles
2 to 8 sprigs fresh cilantro
1 small white onion, chopped or finely sliced
½ cup green onions, finely sliced
1 to 2 cloves garlic, crushed in a garlic press
⅛ to 1 fresh serrano or jalapeño chile, seeded,
        washed, and finely chopped (optional, for a
        spicier dish)
1 cup small, fresh mushroom caps, sliced in half
1 teaspoon fresh thyme, minced
salt and freshly ground pepper

Clean the fish fillets in cold water. Prick both sides of the fish fillets with a fork. Put the wine and 2 tablespoons of lime juice in an ungreased, glass baking dish. Rub the fillets in the marinade to thoroughly coat the fish on both sides. Refrigerate the fish fillets in the marinade for 30 minutes. Turn the fish fillets after 7 minutes. Drain the fish fillets; reserve marinade. Bake the fish fillets on a baking rack in preheated oven for 20 minutes. The fish fillets are done when they flake apart with a fork.

Preheat the broiler. Roast the anaheim chiles 2 to 3 inches under the broiler for 3 to 4 minutes on each side. Occasionally rotate the chiles until they evenly brown and blister on each side. Put the chiles in a tightly closed plastic bag to steam for 5 minutes. Carefully peel off the charred skin. Cut off the stem, seed, rinse, and chop; set aside.

Mince 2 sprigs of cilantro. Sauté the white and green onions, garlic, anaheim and serrano chiles, mushrooms, thyme, and minced cilantro with 2 tablespoons of water in a large skillet over medium-high heat until the onions become tender; stir frequently. Reduce heat to low. Salt and pepper the dish according to individual taste.

Arrange the fish fillets on a serving platter. Attractively cover the fillets with the sautéed onion and mushroom mixture. Garnish with the remaining fresh cilantro sprigs. Sprinkle the remaining 1 tablespoon of lime juice and marinade over the fish. Serve the hot dish immediately.

Serves 6

Each serving provides:

172	Calories	6 g	Carbohydrate
29 g	Protein	143 mg	Sodium
2 g	Fat	72 mg	Cholesterol

97

✦

Mexican Seafood Creole
(Guisado de Mariscos)

Preparation time: 20 minutes
Refrigeration time: 1 hour
Cooking time: 10 to 15 minutes

This seafood recipe blends the unusually exquisite flavors of a spicy, rich red sauce and assorted chunks of fish and shellfish. Such an elegant combination is a festive offering of brilliant colors and textures. Serve this rich, savory dish over rice or noodles to create an attractive and hearty meal. Add more seeds from a jalepeño chile to create an even spicier, livelier seafood dish.

⅓ pound fresh fish fillets, cleaned and cut into
    1-inch pieces
⅓ pound fresh shrimp, peeled, deveined, cleaned,
    and without the tails
½ pound fresh scallops, cleaned in cold water
3 tablespoons lime juice
2 fresh anaheim or poblano chiles
1 medium white onion, chopped or finely
    sliced into rings
½ cup green onions, finely sliced
1 to 2 cloves garlic, crushed in a garlic press
¼ to 2 fresh serrano or jalapeño chiles, seeded,
    washed, and finely sliced
1½ cups Pasilla Chile Sauce (Recipe #20)
1½ cups low-salt broth
1 teaspoon fresh oregano, minced
1 teaspoon fresh thyme, minced

2 sprigs fresh cilantro, minced (optional)
salt and freshly ground pepper

Preheat the broiler. Place the seafood and lime juice in a glass baking dish. Rub the seafood pieces in the marinade to thor-oughly coat the pieces. Cover; refrigerate the seafood in the marinade for 1 hour. Remove the seafood from the marinade; reserve the marinade.

Roast the anaheim chiles 2 to 3 inches under the broiler for 3 to 4 minutes on each side. Occasionally rotate the chiles until they evenly brown and blister on each side. Put the chiles in a tightly closed plastic bag to steam for 5 minutes. Carefully peel off the charred skin. Cut off the stems, seed, rinse, and finely chop.

Sauté the white and green onions, garlic, and serrano and anaheim chiles with 2 tablespoons of water in a large skillet over medium-high heat until the onions become tender; stir frequently. Add the seafood; cook 3 minutes. Mix in the remaining ingredients; reduce heat to low. Cover; simmer the onion and seafood mixture for 10 to 15 minutes. Salt and pepper the dish according to individual taste. Serve the hot seafood creole immediately.

Serves 6

Each serving provides:

109	Calories	11 g	Carbohydrate
16 g	Protein	113 mg	Sodium
1 g	Fat	59 mg	Cholesterol

98

—❧—

Spicy Fish and Rice Stew

(Guisado de Pescado con Arroz)

Preparation time: 20 minutes
Cooking time: 20 to 30 minutes

Such sophisticated flavors as offered by this classic dish
will fulfill the best wishes of all seafood lovers. The deep,
vivid colors and chunks of seafood blend well with ripe,
red tomatoes and chiles. Serve this delightful stew with a
chunk of crusty French bread and a garden-fresh salad
for a magnificent, savory one-dish feast. Served in smaller
portions, this impressive stew is a great opening dish for
an elegant seafood dinner.

1 medium white onion, finely chopped
1/2 cup green onions, finely sliced
1 to 4 cloves garlic, crushed in a garlic press
1/8 to 1 fresh serrano or jalapeño chile, seeded,
    washed, and finely chopped (optional, for a
    spicier dish)
1/3 cup long-grain rice, uncooked
4 medium ripe tomatoes, blanched or roasted,
    peeled, and finely chopped
3 1/2 cups water
1 cup low-salt broth
2 1/2 cups Red Chile Sauce (Recipe #16)
1 tablespoon lime juice
1/2 pound assorted boned, skinless, fresh white fish,
    cut into 1 1/2-inch cubes
1/2 pound fresh scallops, cleaned in cold water
1/4 cup fresh clams or mussels, cleaned in cold water

1 teaspoon fresh oregano, minced
1 bay leaf
2 to 4 sprigs fresh cilantro, minced (optional)
salt and freshly ground pepper

Sauté the white and green onions, garlic, serrano chiles, and rice with 2 tablespoons of water over medium-high heat in a large soup pot until the onions become tender; stir frequently. Stir in the remaining ingredients, excluding the cilantro sprigs. Bring the liquid to a boil; reduce heat to low. Cover; simmer the stew for 20 to 30 minutes until the rice is tender. Salt and pepper the dish according to individual taste. Remove the bay leaf. Serve the hot steaming soup in bowls garnished with the minced cilantro.

Serves 6

Each serving provides:

169	Calories	20 g	Carbohydrate
18 g	Protein	167 mg	Sodium
2 g	Fat	36 mg	Cholesterol

99

—❦—

Salmon Steaks in Green Chile Sauce

(*Salmón en Salsa Verde*)

Preparation time: 20 minutes
Refrigeration time: 30 minutes
Cooking time: 9 minutes

Serve these elegant and sinfully delicious broiled salmon
steaks with a side dish of Mexican-style rice, potatoes, or
noodles and a tossed green dinner salad. For a more
sumptuous, visual feast, serve the salmon steaks atop a
bed of Mexican Green Rice (#57) on a large platter.
Surround the whole platter of rice and fish with crisp,
fresh spinach leaves and assorted greens.

1 fresh anaheim chile
6 small, fresh pink salmon steaks, cleaned, deboned,
    and skinned (about 1½ pounds)
⅓ cup white wine
3 tablespoons lime juice
2¼ cups Green Chile Sauce (Recipe #15)
1 medium white onions, chopped
½ cup green onions, sliced
1 to 2 cloves garlic, crushed in a garlic press
2 to 4 sprigs fresh cilantro, minced (optional)
salt and freshly ground pepper

Preheat the broiler. Roast the anaheim chile 2 to 3 inches
under the broiler for 3 to 4 minutes on each side.
Occasionally rotate the chile until evenly browned and

blistered on each side. Put the chile in a tightly closed plastic bag to steam for 5 minutes. Carefully peel off the charred skin. Cut off the stem, seed, rinse, and finely chop; set aside.

Lightly prick both sides of the salmon steaks with a fork. Combine the wine, lime juice, and $1/4$ cup of the Green Chile Sauce in an ungreased, glass baking dish. Place the salmon steaks in the baking dish and turn them in the marinade to coat both sides thoroughly. Refrigerate the salmon steaks in the marinade for 30 minutes; turn over the steaks after 15 minutes. Drain the marinade from the salmon steaks; reserve.

Sauté the white and green onions, anaheim chiles, and garlic with 2 tablespoons of water in a small saucepan over medium-high heat until the onions become tender; stir frequently. Add the remaining Green Chile Sauce and the cilantro to the cooked onions; reduce the heat to low. Turn on the broiler oven. Place the salmon steaks on a broiler rack atop a baking sheet and brush with the marinade. Broil the salmon steaks 2 to 4 inches below the heat for 4 minutes. Turn the salmon steaks over and brush them with remaining marinade. Continue cooking the salmon steaks 3 to 5 minutes under the broiler until the salmon cooks thoroughly. The salmon steaks are done when they flake apart with a fork.

Combine the remaining marinade with the Green Chile Sauce and onion mixture in the saucepan. Salt and pepper to taste. Arrange the salmon steaks on oven-warmed plates. Attractively place one-sixth portion of the Green Chile Sauce mixture next to each salmon steak. Serve the hot salmon dish immediately.

Serves 6

Each serving provides:

182	Calories	10 g	Carbohydrate
24 g	Protein	101 mg	Sodium
4 g	Fat	59 mg	Cholesterol

100

—✥—

Grilled Shrimp

(Fajitas de Camarones)

Preparation time: 20 minutes
Refrigeration time: 1 hour
Grilling time: 5 minutes
Preheat oven to 350°

Originally made with beef, eager Americans adapted this
popular Mexican *fajita* recipe to include the fruits of the
sea marinaded in lime juice. To enhance this exquisite
feast to perfection, place small serving bowls of shredded
lettuce, chopped tomatoes, chopped jalapeño chiles, salsa,
and lowfat sour cream on the table as condiments for do-
it-yourself serving. If you cannot grill outdoors, broil
these pieces of shrimp 4 to 5 inches under the broiler or in
a cast-iron grill pan.

3 tablespoons lime juice
1 tablespoon water
2 tablespoons apple cider vinegar
1½ pounds raw, fresh jumbo shrimp (24 shrimp),
    peeled, deveined, cleaned, and without the tails
1 fresh anaheim chile
6 fresh lowfat flour tortillas (6-inch)
1 small white onion, halved and finely sliced
½ cup green onions, finely sliced
1 to 2 cloves garlic, crushed in a garlic press
1 small green bell pepper, washed, halved, seeded,
    and finely sliced

1 small yellow bell pepper, washed, halved, seeded,
and finely sliced

1/8 to 1 fresh serrano or jalapeño chile, seeded,
washed, and finely chopped (optional, for a
spicier dish)
salt and freshly ground pepper

Preheat the broiler. Combine the lime juice, water, and
apple cider vinegar in an ungreased, glass baking dish. Rub
the shrimp in the marinade to thoroughly coat the shrimp
in the juices. Cover; marinate the shrimp in the refrigerator
for 1 hour; turn the shrimp pieces occasionally.

Roast the anaheim chile 2 to 3 inches under the
broiler for 3 to 4 minutes on each side. Occasionally
rotate the chile until it evenly browns and blisters on each
side. Put the chile in a tightly closed plastic bag to steam
for 5 minutes. Carefully peel off the charred skin. Cut off
the stem, seed, rinse, and finely chop; set aside.

Wrap tortillas in foil and warm them in preheated
oven for 10 minutes until the tortillas are soft. Remove the
tortillas from the oven; set the foil-wrapped tortillas aside.

Simmer the white and green onions, garlic, green
and yellow bell peppers, and anaheim and serrano chiles
with 2 tablespoons water in a saucepan over medium-high
heat until the onions become tender; stir frequently.
Cook the sautéed mixture for 2 minutes; reduce heat to
low. Salt and pepper the dish according to individual
taste. Remove the shrimp from the marinade; reserve the
marinade.

Skewer the shrimp on metal skewers. Grill the
shrimp for 4 to 5 minutes, occasionally brushing with the
marinade, until the shrimp turns pink on each side.

Place the sautéed onion mixture in a small serving
bowl. Keep the tortillas warm in a covered basket lined
with foil. Remove the shrimp from the skewers and serve
them on an oven-warmed plate, garnished with fresh,
minced cilantro.

To eat the fajitas at the table, open a tortilla and spoon the shrimp, then the tomato and chile mixture down the center of each one. Add the additional condiments as suggested above. Fold the flour tortilla in half or roll it together like a burrito.

Serves 6

Each serving, without condiments, provides:

210	Calories	22 g	Carbohydrate
26 g	Protein	202 mg	Sodium
3 g	Fat	173 mg	Cholesterol

101

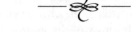

Seafood with Steamed Vegetables
(Mariscos con Verduras)

Preparation time: 35 minutes
Refrigeration time: 45 minutes

Seafood lovers will enjoy this exotic combination of chiles and seafood marinated in white wine and lime juice. The exotic, delicate flavor of the seafood is enhanced by a variety of fresh, colorful steamed vegetables. For variation, you can use octopus, clams, or scallops instead of the squid or shrimp in this recipe. Serve this elegant dish with a fresh garden salad and rice, potatoes, or noodles. You can also reduce portions and serve this delicious recipe as a starter dish for a formal meal.

$1/2$ pound fresh squid, washed and deboned
$1/2$ pound fresh shrimp, peeled, deveined, cleaned,
    and without tails
1 tablespoon white wine
2 tablespoons lime juice
1 tablespoon apple cider vinegar
2 fresh anaheim chiles
2 small white onions, quartered and separated
    into sections
1 small red bell pepper, quartered, seeded, washed,
    and finely sliced
$1/2$ cup snow peas
$1^{1}/2$ cups fresh small mushroom caps, sliced in half

2 medium ripe tomatoes, blanched or roasted,
    peeled, and chopped
1 to 2 cloves garlic, crushed in a garlic press
1/8 to 1 fresh serrano or jalapeño chile, seeded,
    washed, and finely chopped (optional, for a
    spicier dish)
1/2 cup green onions, finely sliced
1 to 3 sprigs fresh cilantro, minced (optional)
1 teaspoon fresh thyme, minced
salt and freshly ground pepper

Preheat the broiler. If the market doesn't clean the squid
for you, here is how to clean the squid at home. Firmly
hold the squid sac down and grasp the end of center
bone. The center bone looks and feels like a clear, hard,
plastic straw. Gently pull the center bone out of the squid.
The head, bone, ink sac, and entrails should also pull
away with the bone. Cut the squid lengthwise. Under
cold, running water, rinse off the skin and clean out the
inside of the squid; dry the squid. With a sharp knife, cut
squid lengthwise into thin, 2 1/2-inch-long strips.

   Place the squid, shrimp, wine, lime juice, and apple
cider vinegar in an ungreased casserole dish. Rub the
seafood pieces in the marinade to thoroughly coat the
seafood. Refrigerate seafood in marinade for 45 minutes.

   Roast the anaheim chiles 2 to 3 inches under the
broiler for 3 to 4 minutes on each side. Occasionally
rotate the chiles until they evenly brown and blister on
each side. Put the chiles in a tightly closed plastic bag to
steam for 5 minutes. Carefully peel off the charred skin.
Cut off the stems, seed, rinse, and finely chop; set aside.

   Place a steamer basket inside a 5-quart pot. Bring
1 inch of water in the pot to the boiling point; reduce heat
to low. Place the white onions, bell pepper, and snow peas
into the pot on the steamer basket. Cook the vegetables,
partially covered, about 3 minutes. Add mushrooms.
Continue steaming vegetables for 4 to 5 minutes until just
tender; set aside.

Sauté the squid, shrimp and marinade in a large skillet over medium-high heat for 4 minutes; stir frequently. Stir in the remaining ingredients; cook for 2 minutes. Remove skillet from heat. Stir in the steamed vegetables; combine well. Salt and pepper the dish according to individual taste. Serve the hot seafood dish immediately.

Serves 6

Each serving provides:

119	Calories	11 g	Carbohydrate
15 g	Protein	85 mg	Sodium
2 g	Fat	145 mg	Cholesterol

Index

International Conversion Chart

These are not exact equivalents: they've been slightly rounded to make measuring easier.

LIQUID MEASUREMENTS

American	Imperial	Metric	Australian
2 tablespoons (1 oz.)	1 fl. oz.	30 ml	1 tablespoon
1/4 cup (2 oz.)	2 fl. oz.	60 ml	2 tablespoons
1/3 cup (3 oz.)	3 fl. oz.	80 ml	1/4 cup
1/2 cup (4 oz.)	4 fl. oz.	125 ml	1/3 cup
2/3 cup (5 oz.)	5 fl. oz.	165 ml	1/2 cup
3/4 cup (6 oz.)	6 fl. oz.	185 ml	2/3 cup
1 cup (8 oz.)	8 fl. oz.	250 ml	3/4 cup

SPOON MEASUREMENTS

American	Metric
1/4 teaspoon	1 ml
1/2 teaspoon	2 ml
1 teaspoon	5 ml
1 tablespoon	15 ml

WEIGHTS

US/UK	Metric
1 oz.	30 grams (g)
2 oz.	60 g
4 oz. (1/4 lb)	125 g
5 oz. (1/3 lb)	155 g
6 oz.	185 g
7 oz.	220 g
8 oz. (1/2 lb)	250 g
10 oz.	315 g
12 oz. (3/4 lb)	375 g
14 oz.	440 g
16 oz. (1 lb)	500 g
2 lbs	1 kg

OVEN TEMPERATURES

Farenheit	Centigrade	Gas
250	120	1/2
300	150	2
325	160	3
350	180	4
375	190	5
400	200	6
450	230	8